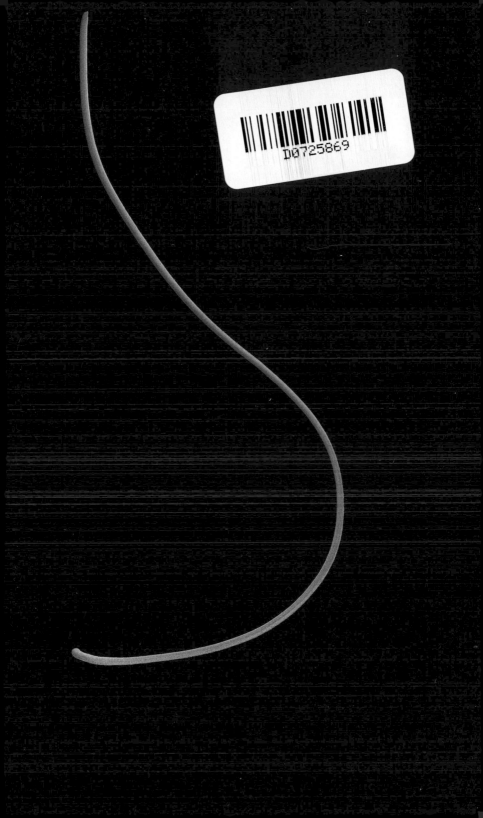

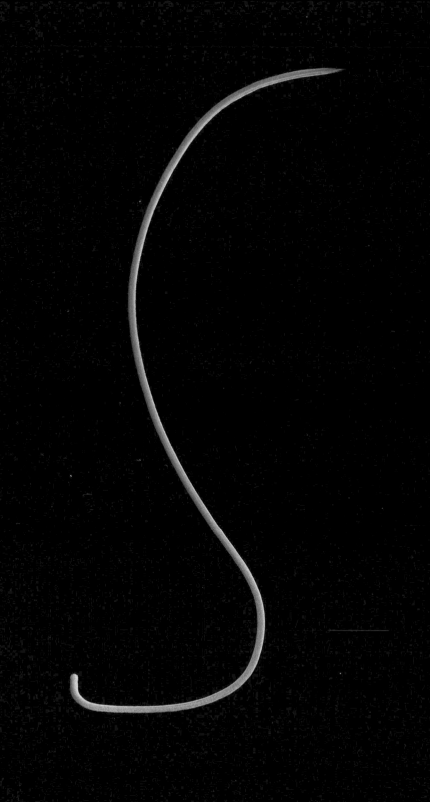

CALIGULA
DIVINE CARNAGE

Credits

CALIGULA: DIVINE CARNAGE
by
Stephen Barber & Jeremy Reed
ISBN 1 84068 049 0
A Creation Book
First published 2001
Copyright © Creation Books 2000
Foreword copyright © James Havoc 1999
All world rights reserved
Design, typesetting:
PCP International, Bradley Davis
A Butcherbest Production

CALIGULA
DIVINE CARNAGE

ATROCITIES OF THE ROMAN EMPERORS

STEPHEN BARBER · JEREMY REED

CONTENTS

Foreword
Orgy Of Death
James Havoc
5

Introduction
Purple Haze: Decadence, Derangement, Depravity
Jeremy Reed
11

One
Caligula: Divine Carnage
Stephen Barber
23

Two
Gladiator: Blood, Semen, Ecstasy
Stephen Barber
59

Three
Commodus: Imperial Delirium
Stephen Barber
93

Four
Heliogabalus: Black Sun Rising
Jeremy Reed
107

Postscript
"Ultima Verba": The Final Atrocity
Stephen Barber
153

Index
157

FOREWORD:
ORGY OF DEATH

Ever since the cinematic holocaust of Tinto Brass' blood-splattered porno epic *Caligula* in 1980, connoisseurs of visceral history have thirsted for more information and details on the pleasuredomes and necrodromes of Ancient Rome. Yet the true glories of the Roman Empire – the slaughter, the sexual depravity, the insanity – were virtually impossible to glean from the handful of arid, academic texts available. Finally, here is a book which *counts* – a book which pointedly eschews the mind-numbing minutiae of politico-military history and instead brings the glorious, often shocking decadence of Ancient Rome to bloody, pulsating life.

Here are the incredible cruelties, vices and vanities of emperors such as Caligula and Claudius [see Chapter One], Nero [see Chapter Four], Commodus [see Chapter Three] and Heliogabalus [see Chapter Four] in uncensored and vivid relief.

Although Augustus, the first emperor, was a model of decency and restraint, his successor Tiberius (emperor from AD 14–37), notoriously set the tone for imperial debauch in his latter years, when he retired to Capri in around AD 30 [see also Chapter One]. Here, he surrounded himself with young male concubines and indulged in endless orgies of sodomy, cock-sucking and coprophilia. It is reported that the walls of his villa were daubed with vast and complex pornographic friezes which would have shamed de Sade. Not content with enticing mullet to nibble his crumb-coated genitals as he reclined in the tepid rock pools, Tiberius was also in the habit of glazing his penis with milk and honey so that unweaned babes would eagerly suckle at his glans, innocently guzzling the old wretch's torpid emissions.

Yet the excesses and vices of the more infamous tyrants were often matched by lesser known monsters such as Vitellius, whose brief 9-month reign was marked by gluttony, sloth and cowardice and ended in him being hideously tortured and butchered, and then hurled bit by bit into the River Tiber. Vitellius, one of the hundreds of boy prostitutes under Tiberius in Capri, went on to work as courier/catamite for Caligula, Claudius and Nero in turn, and had become emperor by default in AD 69, following the respective decapitation and suicide of Galba and Otho, Nero's transitory successors.

Then there was Domitian, emperor from AD 81–96[1], who favoured freaks and was always accompanied to the games by a stunted, gibbering pinhead draped in drool-streaked purple robes. Domitian even bought and trained his own legion of achondroplasic dwarf gladiators, who he sent into the arena to combat topless, ferocious female fighters armed with tridents in grotesque and bloody gavottes of death. Attributed with great phallic power, these dwarfs were watched in naked training by the finest ladies in Rome, who coveted their out-sized generative members.[2]

Domitian meanwhile lusted after prostitutes and courtesans without surcease, and delighted in depilating their lubricious pubic mounds by hand-held tweezers before penetration. Rumours of his incest and pederasty abounded. With gleeful hypocrisy he also inflicted awful punishments on the Vestal Virgins, burying the Chief Virgin alive for the sin of fornication and having her lovers horse-whipped to a bloody pulp in the Forum (a tradition upheld by later brutes such as Caracalla [see Chapter Three], who executed four Vestals in this manner during his murderous regime). Domitian also added refinements to the torture of Christians and other fringe cultists, introducing the insertion of burning reeds into the glans penis and localized immolation of the testicles in reprisal for their lunatic heresies.[3] Always in dread of assassination – he even lined the imperial palace with mirrored marble so he could see behind him at all times – he finally inaugurated a vicious, paranoiac pre-emptive killing program in AD 93 that lasted for over two years; senators, officers and family members alike were poisoned or put to sword until Domitian himself was hacked to bloody fragments by conspirators, to be remembered with the same fearful disdain as Tiberius or Caligula by future generations[4].

Yet these purple, gore-tainted snapshots are but a taste of the delights and delirium to follow. Whether your appetite for carnage on a grand scale was whetted by *Caligula*, or even perhaps by the more recent *Gladiator* with its leering depiction of Commodus, in the ensuing pages you will surely find true and lasting satiety.

—James Havoc

1. Vitellius had been succeeded as emperor in AD 69 by Vespasian, who died from a torrential, bowel-shredding diarrhoea attack after drinking tainted spring water, and in AD 79 by the unpopular Titus, a shameless libertine noted only for his nocturnal debauches with catamites and sperm-drinking eunuchs, who also fell foul of disease and expired in a welter of blood-streaked malarial vomit (it is also reported that Domitian, to usher Titus on his way to hell, had his death-bed packed with ice and snow).

2. Freak culture thrived throughout the centuries of Empire; dwarfs of either sex could be purchased in the Forum Morionium and female hunchbacks, cripples or pinheads were much sought-after as concubines. Magicians and soothsayers would oft cause freaks to be disembowelled alive, divining the future by sifting through many a deformed set of steaming, uncoiling viscera. Augustus, the very first emperor, had a pet dwarf named Lucius, and many of his successors similarly enjoyed the company of human anomalies at imperial court or in their harems. Caligula reputedly gave his slavering retinue of dwarf clowns the absolute power over life and death. It is also reported that the Romans did not hesitate to create and nurture such creatures by brutally contorting, snapping or severing the limbs of infants.

3. It was Domitian who perpetrated the second major persecution of the Christians, following in the footsteps of Nero who, seeking scapegoats for the Great Fire of Rome in AD 64 – which many believed to have been started by Nero himself in order to clear land for his enormous new palace and grounds, the Golden House – inaugurated the first of many brutal mass purges against this insurgent monotheistic cult. Nero had thousands of them severely tortured, dressed in the skins of wild beasts and finally either torn to shreds by starving mastiffs or tied to stakes and crosses and set on fire while still alive, making screaming human torches to illuminate the streets and arenas of Rome by night. Although Christians had fallen foul of previous emperors in smaller numbers (Caligula favoured profound facial disfigurement by branding-iron and sawing in half), a pattern for their relentless mass murder was now established, and flourished through subsequent years of Empire marked by such notable peaks of ferocity as the capture and execution of Saint Blandina and her followers in AD 177, at about the time of the accession of the Emperor Commodus. This atrocity occurred at Lyons, where Christians found themselves at odds with the Roman cult of Cybele. In 177 the Christian Easter clashed with the orgiastic Cybeleian rites; it was the perfect excuse for another purge. Blandina and her followers were tracked down, captured, and put to a slow death in the arena over six days. Stripped naked and bound to stakes, the Christians were exposed to the mauling of wild beasts of every description, so that the skin and meat was gradually eaten or clawed away from their bones as they clung to the hideous vestiges of life. Many of these beasts were

specially trained to sexually violate and sodomize their prey before dismemberment; female prisoners doused in civet grease were often raped half to death by feral dogs or buggered by baboons beneath the spectators' gaze, before being duly devoured. Blandina herself, after a prolonged labial mangling, was hurled into a huge frying-pan of boiling oil and half cooked. Then she was wrapped in a net and thrown before wild bulls; finally, after being trampled and gored to the point of extinction, her throat was cut from ear to ear and spinal cord severed.

Being eaten alive by hungry wild animals was not the worst fate to befall a Christian, however; other cruelties traditionally inflicted on the Christian "martyrs" included all types of crucifixion, such as being nailed to a cross with arms outstretched or suspended upside-down, where victims were either left to a slow painful death, hacked apart, or burnt alive. Similar to this was impalement by a sharpened stake, usually through the entrails via the rectum. Victims bound to stakes could be pierced by arrows or spears, or have the meat flayed from their living bones by iron claws and spikes. Women would be hung by the hair, and their breasts were often hacked off. Virgins were always raped by their executioner before the kill. Anointing the face or genitals with honey was another method, so the victim would be stung or bitten to death by insects, usually with great lead weights attached to every limb. Hanging by one foot or arm, or even by the thumbs, was also common. Heads were pounded with hammers, kneecaps pulverized, lungs choked by pyres of burning excrement.

Other victims were clamped into wooden barrels, with only head, hands and feet exposed, and force-fed milk and honey, the same mixture being coated over their skin. Tormented by insects on the outside, the victim's innards would meanwhile erupt with noxious liquid excrement flexing with intestinal worms. Death could take up to two weeks, the wretched Christian's flesh rotting away in its own filth and devoured by all manner of parasites. A similar fate was to be stitched inside a gutted animal skin, with only head exposed, and left in the blazing sun. The victim's blood would nearly boil, his or her body gnawed by maggots and gouged by the beaks of vultures.

Christians were also chained to great wooden wheels and their bodies shattered with hammers; they were crushed in great vises; they were torn, ripped and stabbed by rotating metal wheels edged with blades; they were stretched on racks until their limbs ripped away and their innards burst out; they were hung up by manacles or neck-collars and their limbs were dislocated or smashed; they were whipped with flails and cudgels, torn with pincers, hooks and iron claws, skinned alive and roasted in frying-pans or between red-hot iron plates; boiling oil or lead was poured over them, their limbs were chopped off, their genitals were pulped, they were buggered to death with huge, serrated metal dildos; they were stoned, drowned, buried alive, hurled into ravines, or simply beheaded.

Fire was a favourite weapon of torture. Saint Antipas was sealed into a bronze horse and cooked; Saint Euphemia was dismembered and forced to watch her own limbs sizzle in a great pan; Saint Laurence perished on a red-hot griddle; and Saint Cyrilla's belly was slit open, and red-hot coals piled over her entrails. Eyes were burnt out with firebrands, feet cooked in red-hot metal shoes, brains roasted inside burning helmets, flesh seared away from limbs leaving victims to writhe in agony with their charred and smoking bones exposed.

Saint Eucratia had her liver torn out and eaten raw; Saint Prisca was ripped open and her belly stuffed with wild barley to be eaten by hogs; Saint Laurus was eviscerated by a caustic quicklime enema; Saint Febronia had her teeth pulled out and tongue fed to mastiffs; Saint Severus's lips were sliced off and shoved into his anus; and Saint Fausta was pierced with nails then slowly sawn in half, lengthwise, with her vulva as the starting-groove. The list is endless; the tortures inflicted on the Christians were legendary and legion, a catalogue of atrocity only rivalled, perhaps, by the sado-masochistic excesses of the Roman gladiatorial games themselves [see Chapter Two].

4. The death of Domitian inaugurated a period of nearly one hundred years when the Roman Empire stabilised to a degree, being ruled in turn by the peaceful Nerva, the great soldier Trajan, cultured but eccentric Hadrian, steady and boring Antonius Pius, and then the joint emperors Marcus Aurelius and Lucius Verus (the latter always overshadowed by his co-ruler's military exploits). Then, in AD 180, the madness returned with a vengeance – in the vainglorious form of Commodus.

INTRODUCTION
PURPLE HAZE: DECADENCE, DERANGEMENT, DEPRAVITY

"The object of their toil was their epitaph"
—Seneca

What is it about the decadent bloodline of Roman emperors –
amongst whom we include Tiberius, Caligula, Nero, Domitian,
Commodus, Caracalla and Heliogabalus (the more popular name
of Elagabalus) – that has continued over the centuries to impose
an indelible fingerprint on time?

Is it a fascination with their propensity for self-
deification that finds in their uncompromising extravagance an
interface with the rock-gods of the twentieth century? Are their
various pathologies, homicidal rages and obsessive manias the
template for a Jungian-based archetypal psychology? Isn't their
tyrannical despotism repeated in the drive-unit awakened in
each new political dictator? And hasn't their histrionic love of
transvestism and unashamed polysexual experimentation served
as a colourful model for all those who incline to a flexible use of
gender (Heliogabalus as we know it, wanted to be castrated and
fitted with an artificial vagina and to become a full transsexual,
but was denied the request by his surgeons)? And what of their
predilection for excess, be it orgiastic, gourmet, or acquisitive in
their love of jewels, fabrics and the adoption of creatures like
leopards and panthers as exotic pets? Haven't we known these
psychological traits repeated in the behaviour of the glitterati
both in our own time and through historic examples? Isn't the

mad-emperor archetype a sequence programmed into the collective psyche?

It's a long way back in time to the Julio-Claudian dynasty, and the deranged emperors Caligula and Nero, but only if we conceive of time as a linear concept, rather than as a spatial one conducting repeat psychic happenings, themselves modified by social update. Nothing is old and nothing is new: what we experience are variants of the phenomenon Jung called psychological types. By this I mean that the psycho-organic dysfunctions inherent in Caligula are immediate rather than historic, his possible schizophrenia a state analagous to the delusional rage to be witnessed in the outcasts of today's society.

Yet in the case of the mad Caesars the situation was radically different. The unlimited resources of power and wealth at their disposal, and the belief in their own incorrigible status as demi-gods allowed them to act out their pathologies in a way that was perversely inhuman. Caligula we are told so loved wealth that he literally rolled on heaps of gold, and had a life-size statue of himself constructed from his favourite metal. Vitellius gave the Imperial Navy the task of searching the seas to provide him with rare sea-food delicacies. Vitellius, whose gustatory quirks extended to a fondness for pike livers, pheasant brains and flamingo tongues, once staged a banquet involving a select 2,000 fish and 7,000 birds. Domitian would stage dinner-parties in which all the food eaten was black, and so too the plates on which it was served (an idea later incorporated by the novelist J.K. Huysmans into his fictional synthesis of decadence, *A Rebours*).

The exhibitionistic Heliogabalus would not only make-up as a woman, but would work as a prostitute himself in some of the city's most notorious brothels. Caligula, to boost his claims to divinity, ordered the construction of a three-miles-long bridge of boats across the Bay of Naples, and crossed them on horseback, wearing the breastplate of Alexander the Great. Caligula's claim was that, like the sea-god Neptune, he had ridden over and conquered the waters. Commodus would slaughter ostriches all afternoon in the amphitheatre to the applause of his subjects, and then proclaim himself an insuperable conqueror, a protégé of Hercules.

These manifestations of megalomania were of course in part condoned by a decadent society grown used to aberrant sexual practices and the vicious caprices of its mad emperors. But it would be wrong to assume that the atrocities committed by the emperors were sanctioned by their subjects. Caligula, who was sensitive about his premature baldness, would demand on seeing someone with a fine head of hair that he or she be shaved on the spot, and Heliogabalus was to outrage the Senate by going through a marriage ceremony with a man. These are isolated incidents of megalomania that went deep into collective resentment, and which would contrive in time to have the offending emperors usurped and murdered. It was the solid muscle of the Roman army, tempered by a healthy realisation in its leaders that the depredations of a mad emperor would like cancer cells threaten the imperial organism as a whole, that invariably checked individual tyranny by assassination. The psychotic, the schizophrenic, the paranoid, the deviant and the socially maladjusted are the dominants in any psychosexual study of the more extreme aspects of the decadent emperors – decadent implying living outside the strictures usually imposed on people by the apprehension of conforming to a given social ethos. Decadence as a psychological trait usually implies the subversion of moral restraint by an attenuated sensory aesthetic. What any decadent lineage shares in common is the ability to address the present as a total state of being. By magnifying the moment, and living within its register, rather than with the promise of an illusory future, the decadent sensibility succeeds in maximizing immediate sensation. And for the emperors Nero, Tiberius, Caligula and Heliogabalus, immediacy was not only a reminder of their privileged incarnation, but also the oppositional thrust to their acute awareness of threatened mortality. By their outrages against humanity, their exaggerated sexual fetishes and their total disdain for compromise, the decadent lineage short-circuited any prospects of individual longevity.

The perverse emperors lived not only with the knowledge that they would in all probability be assassinated, but they were also immersed in a culture of death. There was not only the brutal carnage of war, but there was the amphitheatre in which both humans and animals were slaughtered, and there were capricious executions carried out at the emperor's command. Death was present in every aspect of living. That it could come at any moment, and very often by violent means, led in turn to the privileged cultivating a world of decadent excess by way of compensation for their continuously ruptured lives. The historian Aelius Lampridius tells us in his *Scriptores Historu Augustu* that the emperor Heliogabalus prepared a whole death-kit in anticipation of committing suicide with the same extravagant gestures as he had lived. Thinking that he might hang himself, Heliogabalus prepared a noose in which the cords were interwoven with purple and scarlet silk. In addition he kept pure gold swords with which to stab himself should violence impend. And in keeping with his inordinate love of jewels, he had designed for him a number of poison rings capped by sapphires, emeralds and ceraunites. Heliogabalus was denied access to his pre-arranged means of suicide by the sudden manner of his assassination, but what is significant here is the ritualised ways in which he intended to meet his death. The youthful Heliogabalus with all his effete, self-dramatising gestures must have felt fractionally safer in the knowledge that he could impose control over his death by a spectacularly orchestrated suicide.

Like Heliogabalus, Caligula too had a theatrical interest in dramatising aspects of himself both inwardly and outwardly. Caligula's passion for the stage was such that he presented constant *ludi scaenici*, some of them at night, when he would have the entire city lit to accommodate the actors. Caligula not only formed friendships with Apelles, the most famous actor of his day, but also with the pantomime Mnester, and is reported to have had sexual relations with both men. Caligula's identification with theatre can be seen as a form of psycho-drama, a way of attaching his inner status of self-deification to a legitimate external source. Caligula's life was also a rehearsal for death, and within the arena of his psyche he must have constantly played and replayed the variants of his possible assassination. Men who live by blood learn the dialectic of preparing to die by blood. Caligula was butchered in a tunnel leading from the forum, on his way to congratulate three Asian boys who had themselves just survived the performance of a gore-drenched dance of death.

      The emperor Nero shared pathological strains in common with both Caligula and Heliogabalus, and conducted spurious marriages to his homosexual lovers Pythagoras and Sporus, the latter a boy whom he had castrated. The desire for gender substitution and the attempt to transsexualize male into female, was a component of the decadent sensibility that asserted a powerful fascination over both Nero and Heliogabalus. If we read the concept of transsexuality as a desire on the individual's part to recreate gender without acknowledgement to parents, then we can link the psychological notions of the act to the belief common among the emperors in their extraordinary incarnations as self-proclaimed deities. The omnipotence invested in the measure of being god-like is not dissimilar from the state realised by the transsexual in changing sex. Both conditions deny genetic parentage and seek to qualify rebirth as a social identity, and both are roles involving radical non-conformist individuation. To imagine what it must have been like to live in the minds of Tiberius, Caligula, Commodus, Nero or Heliogabalus, we have to let go the premises of innate social preconditioning that colours our behaviour with others. For the mad emperors discussed in this study compromise was not an option. To live in a world dictated by obsession, compulsion and private fantasies bordering on the psychotic is one thing, but to have the power to externalize and act out these promptings is another. The instinctual monitoring of emotions, a mechanism which allows humans to interact socially was something rarely observed by the megalomaniac emperors. For them the barrier between inner and outer realities was precariously fragile, and often not observed at all.

Commodus, another of the decadent emperors to identify with the Greek god Hercules, had statues cast of himself wearing the distinctive herculean lion skin, while in his right hand he held a knotted club. Commodus's desire to prove himself a marksman led him to perform in the arena during the Plebeian Games of November 192. According to Cassius Dio who was an eye-witness to the event: "On the first day he killed a hundred bears all by himself, shooting down at them from the railing of the walkway... On the other days he fought domestic animals in the arena. He also killed a tiger, a hippopotamus and an elephant. Having performed these exploits, he would retire, but later, after luncheon, he would fight as a gladiator. The form of contest that he practised and the armour that he used were those of the 'secutores'... he held the shield in his right hand and the wooden sword in his left, and indeed took great pride in the fact that he was left-handed."

Commodus, who was less interested in imperial government than he was in the pursuit of personal obsessions, was said to have had a harem of 300 concubines and 300 young boys, many of whom had been bought for the purposes of his sexual pleasure. Commodus seems like most of the later emperors to have been bisexual and to have been sufficiently adept at maintaining an interest in both sexes, as not to arouse the Senate's indignation. In the triumphal rites of his accession, Commodus struck up immediate controversy by seating his favourite Saoterus in the imperial chariot, and by amorously kissing him from time to time during the proceedings. This act of defiant homoeroticism was a signal that Commodus intended to impose no constraint on the overlap between private and public interests. The demand later in his reign that the Senate deify him as a living god, and by the name of Hercules son of Zeus, was further confirmation of the delusions entertained by Commodus in the breakdown of his communications with reality. Like Heliogabalus, who would debase himself by working in disguise as a rent boy, Commodus got his kicks by identifying with gladiators who were among the most despised classes of ancient Rome. By taking part in the gladiatorial games

Commodus brought opprobrium to his elevated title. But it's easy to see how both emperors should have come to empathise with the socially despised: rent boys and gladiators. It's more than possible that both Heliogabalus and Commodus felt most liberated when identifying with their social opposites. Given the autocratic power at the disposal of a Nero, a Caligula, or a Commodus, the autonomous wish to invest in the characteristics of a particular god, a hero, or a vilified member of society was something immediately realisable.

The polymorphic character tendencies shared by the more extreme Caesars, while they point up constituents common to both schizophrenia and psychosis, were also an inventive theatre of inner play. Archetypal imagination by reason of its orientation to myth, and the whole mythopoetic cosmos is also the vehicle that shapes metamorphosis. Ovid's idea of the magical alteration of physical form from one species to another, and of the gods having an active part in the process was a way of channelling poetic imagination into a series of fluently mutating archetypes. Ovid who had lived at the time of Julius Caesar, and who was exiled in later life to the island of Tomis in the Black Sea for some unexplained offence to the great leader, was arguably the poet who by drawing on the configurative resources available to the imagination came nearest to writing a psychological poetry. In discovering a universalised metaphor for imaginal states Ovid was undoubtedly aware of the important role metamorphosis played within the arena of the psyche. When Suetonius relates that Nero raped the Vestal Virgin Rubria, or Tiberius had a centurion flogged to within inches of his life for failing to prevent a minor diversion in the emperor's progress, we are in apprehending the instantaneous perversion of these acts, close to the subject of metamorphosis. In these instances a violent physical transformation was effected by sadistic agencies. It was the capriciousness and unpredictability of how the emperor would relate to an event, be it good or bad, that had imperial behaviour register within the framework of metamorphosis. Again it is Suetonius who provides the narrative relating to an act of repellent savagery on

Tiberius's part, while he was resident on Capri. A fisherman hoping to please the emperor intruded on his solitude by presenting him with an enormous mullet. Not in the least flattered by the gift Tiberius ordered that the fish should be de-scaled by being rubbed in the man's face. When the fisherman in his agony shouted out that it was as well that he hadn't presented Caesar with a huge crab he had caught, Tiberius sent for the crab and had it used in the same way. He also had the mullet rammed deep into the man's rectum.

Such acts of despotic savagery, unmediated as they were by any consideration for the victim suggest a dangerous interaction between impulse and its conversion to action. One could argue that the speed with which this transaction of energies takes place is metamorphic in its intensity. Ovid had introduced his epic poem with the intention "to tell of bodies changed into new forms". He might equally have stated his aim as the instruction of one psychological state as it colours another. The complex mechanism of change and the new form imparted by that transformation is essential to Ovid's method. But by transferring the poet's conversion of energies from a mythic to a psychological plane, we can see how well the pattern fits with the impulsive behaviour governing the late emperors. When Caligula's homosexual favourite, Mnester the comedian, was performing in the theatre, Caligula would personally beat with his hands any offender who made the least noise during the performance. The premise of violence here of course hinges on the notion of non-retaliation, and of a tyrannical outburst on the emperor's part being allowed to complete itself in the manner of desire complemented by action. The metamorphic valency of the act permits of no interruption in the consummation of a fantasy. In normal life one individual who is aggravated by another is usually forced to take revenge by way of internalising anger. The imagined confrontation should it grow into a reality would involve opposition on the other's part and the possibility of intervention by the law. Social man is forced to curtail instinctual anger, whereas a Caligula or a Tiberius could inflict any atrocity they chose on a necessarily passive recipient.

It was William Blake, who within the context of poetic idealism, wrote, "Sooner murder an infant in its cradle than nurse unacted desires". While Blake's intentions in this particular proverb were in the interests of unmediated truth, he would doubtless have refrained from acting out the physicalization of a provocatively tuned metaphysical dictum. Revolutionary as they were, Blake's political concerns at the time of writing *The Marriage Of Heaven And Hell* were very different from the obsession with unrestrained power entertained by the Roman emperors. The emperor qualified his actions by an inner contract and not by the reflective quality that usually tempers instinct. Given to primitive forms of vatic enquiry over their individual destinies, like the inspection of fresh entrails, or divinations through prophecy, the emperors lived in a world of ritualised fetish and fertilely protean superstition. In most instances their inner preoccupations became politicised, leading to the breakdown of objective rationale, and the intrusion of subjective bias in place of considered decisions.

In many ways the prototypical icons of the decadent imagination, the mad emperors with their devotion to excess have been kept alive in the archetypal underworld of the collective unconscious. Antonin Artaud's powerfully imagined recreation of the life of Heliogabalus, via the Roman historian Aelius Lampridius, is one instance of a creative artist reincarnating a spectacularly unorthodox predecessor through the medium of empathy. Artaud's affinities with magical-religious systems, and his cutting-edge devotion to translating the self into unmediated imaginative expression provided the ideal basis for the meeting of two revolutionary sensibilities on a psychic plane. Artaud's *Heliogabalus or The Anarchist Crowned* (1934) is a supreme imaginative fiction, and one which allows Artaud to revision history by rediscovering the read out of his subject's inner dynamic. By deconstructing the defences of his historic sources Artaud was able to retrieve Heliogabalus as a live, capricious entity. Historians often attempt to impose a linear structure on events that happened like a series of speeded-up, disconnected film-frames. Artaud tells us something very important about Heliogabalus, and that is his conversion of imperial power into theatre. Artaud's method of revisioning, rather than narrating his subject, allows him to establish the correlation between poetry and revolution vital to the understanding of Heliogabalus's anarchic conduct. "Exactly what did Heliogabalus do?" Artaud questions, before affirming that the emperor "may have transformed the Roman throne into a stage, but in so doing he introduced theatre and, through theatre, poetry to the throne of Rome, into the palace of the Roman emperor, and poetry, when it is real, is worthy of blood, it justifies the shedding of blood".

This is not a sentiment that Lampridius would have arrived at, but it is one that helps explain the gestural histrionics that were at the core of Heliogabalus's theatrical behaviour. Artaud's realisation that real poetry justifies bloodshed is a perception that helps extend our knowledge of this youthfully deviant emperor, and so provides an update on someone straitjacketed by historic account. Artaud's recreation of Heliogabalus is a model of inventive history, by which I mean one that looks to imagination as its source, and so liberates its subject from received facts.

Artaud in his study of Heliogabalus draws extensively on the emperor's immersion in the mythopoetic. Artaud calls Heliogabalus "a mythomaniac in the literal and concrete sense of the word. Which is to say that he saw the myths that existed, and applied them. He applied for once, and perhaps the only time in history, myths that were true". The ability to live within the immediacy of myth, and to know the mythopoetic within the context of concrete reality was a level of consciousness shared by some of the extreme psychologies that make up any study of decadent sensibility. The making of psychic reality is an imaginative process, and one rooted in the archetypally-based premises of the psyche. Now it is the play of psychological ambivalence in our inner activities, or what Jung called "an inherent tension of opposites" that allows us to experience the multiple patterns coded into the unconscious. Duplicity, or the possibility of acting out our opposite or shadow is a potential reality that we instinctually depathologize. But for a Caligula or a Heliogabalus operating within the context of mythic reality the opposite was a dictate as much to be spontaneously obeyed as that of the motive to do good. Both options were integrated into sensibilities motivated by the concept of omnipotent heroism and the rites of self-deification. Heliogabalus's behaviour remained unedited by social compromise because his role was that of a participant in myth. Artaud's twentieth-century contention that capitalist society deliberately represses the individual's inner growth was to have him sectioned for much of his adult life. If Artaud's life was consigned to the continuous polemic of giving artistic expression to his inner theatre of imagination, then he was forced to suffer a frustration that would have been unknown to Heliogabalus. Artaud's agonised suffering was compounded of the realisation that man had become demythicized at the expense of manipulative ideologies. Artaud's search for the primal within himself took him to Heliogabalus and the latter's association with sun-worship and the celebratory rites of transcendent imagination.

The decadent Roman emperors continue to live on in the underground precincts of the psyche. Their psychological rebirth is continuous, and it is one that must be met by imaginative rather than historic thinking. What did it feel like to have absolute power over the lives of your subjects, with all their hopes, fears, vulnerability, loves and individual destinies likely to be extinguished by a perverse quirk of unpredictable anger? Was remorse a part of this ostentatious murder-package? We know that insomnia and livid, cinematic dreams pursued Nero after he had embarked on a chain of family murders. Although incidents of stingingly painful flashbacks as a part of psychological nemesis went largely unrecorded by contemporary historians, Nero and Tiberius in particular manifested powerful guilt symptoms, with Tiberius actually renouncing his despotism in a series of letters to the Senate.

What do people do after committing atrocities? Is there a rupture in their ongoing lives characterised by depression, disorientation or agonised introversion? That the emperors under scrutiny in this book were probably none of them pure psychopaths suggests that there was an emotional input into crimes committed, and a corresponding subjective identification with the act. We're told little of their ability to evaluate the good and the bad in themselves, or of the personal terror that must have invaded their private hours. If, as Artaud implies, their atrocities were condoned by the emperor's embodying the rites of mythic consciousness, then their superiority depended upon shocking the collective into an awareness of divine prerogative. Moral exemption from being personally accountable for crime is one definition of megalomania, and madness another. Somewhere between these two polarities we encounter the manias and psychological extremes of the autocratic Caesars of Rome.

CHAPTER ONE
CALIGULA:
DIVINE CARNAGE

In the great annals of atrocity, the reign of the Roman emperor Caligula glares out with acetylene brilliance and splendour. Unlike the acts of almost every other autocrat in the black history of mass slaughter, Caligula's tyranny was executed with a supreme deviance and caprice, staged as a vast performance of bestiality, brutality, sexual excess and perversion, for the edification of his largely adoring subjects. The brevity of Caligula's position as the ruler of the known world accentuated the monstrous intensity of his outrages, allowing them to serve as an exemplary inspiration for the infinite acts of atrocity committed by despotic regimes over the following two millennia. But, however hard they tried to emulate him, no subsequent dictator or tyrant has ever succeeded in saturating the institutions of power with indignity and infamy in the way that Caligula did. It was a world-shattering achievement. The nonchalant way in which Caligula planned to irreparably implode the Roman Empire – and, as the icing on the cake, hand the broken pieces on to a drooling cretin – demonstrates the futility and horror of power to its maximal degree. But it was a performance which cost Caligula his life, in a blood-sodden denouement that was his final, and greatest, act.

Gaius Julius Caesar Germanicus was born in Anzio, on the Mediterranean coast, on 31 August AD 12. As a child, his father, Germanicus – a celebrated warrior who was a likely contender for the role of emperor – took the child with him on his military campaign against the unruly Teutonic hordes, along the banks of the river Rhine. It was there, in the brutish camps of the Roman legions, where buggery ruled supreme, that the boy was given his affectionate nickname, "Caligula" – "Little Boots" – after the military-style footwear which he had to wear in the perpetually muddy conditions of the sordid camps. The nickname stuck, even though Caligula detested it, and he would ironically pass into history with an anodyne soubriquet which was the utter contradiction of the lethal devastation that he unleashed upon the Roman world and its enemies, and ultimately upon himself.

Caligula's childhood saw an entire catalogue of murders, exiles and bestial humiliations inflicted on those around him. Almost every member of his family had been surreptitiously murdered or tortured into extinction by the time he became emperor. Although he would become only the third of the Julio-Claudian emperors, the dynasty was already tainted with an indelible malediction by the time of Caligula's accession, and had definitively run aground in a morass of corruption, incest, child sex and mass executions. Although the first Julio-Claudian emperor, Augustus, was still alive at the time of Caligula's birth, he expired two years later and was succeeded by his adopted son, Tiberius, who was already elderly. Although Tiberius proved to be an adept administrator and military planner, the Empire veered off into disarray under his rule. Tiberius preferred to reign from outside Rome, since he loathed the plebeian scum of the city with absolute ferocity. Although his own life was marked by excess and deviance – he was a sexual pervert of the highest order, who refined sophisticated mixtures of butchery and lust within the confines of his lavish palaces – Tiberius preferred to appear as an austere autocrat to his subjects, and rationed their own pleasures rigorously. The plebeian scum of Rome lived for the ecstatic sensations of the arena and the spectacles of gladiatorial slaughter which were staged there. Tiberius reduced the number of great festivals in the arena to an absolute minimum, and almost never took his assigned place to watch the slaughter along with his subjects. As a result, he was detested. For the last decade of his reign,

Tiberius mainly lived in his palace on the island of Capri, off the Mediterranean coast, where he could simultaneously be protected from assassination by the plebeian multitude or by other enemies of his icy power, and also pursue his old man's obsessions with the laceration and multiple penetration of youthful sexual organs.

Tiberius arranged for the poisoning and murders of Caligula's father and two brothers, and exiled his mother to a remote island where she committed suicide in despair. All of those deaths formed part of the intricate power regime instituted by Tiberius, conceived in order to annihilate threats to his imperial status (Caligula's father Germanicus had been far more popular than Tiberius) and to try to arrange the future of the Empire in his own image. But he overdid his campaigns of slaughter, to the point where only Caligula – who, without those multiple murders, would never have become a contender for emperor – and Tiberius's young grandson Gemellus survived from the near-decimated Julio-Claudian dynasty. The only other, and much more remote, contender was the hapless cretin Claudius, Caligula's uncle, whom the family had always tried to hide from public view. Caligula was an excitable and vindictive child, who was psychotically inclined from birth and subsequently traumatized still further by the executions of the male members of his family. He became increasingly attached to his three sisters, especially the beautiful Drusilla, three years younger than himself; although Caligula committed incest with all of his sisters, it was Drusilla, then fourteen years of age, who became the primary focus of Caligula's sexual obsession. The four children were shifted around from one house to another in Rome, and for years on end, their fearful lives hung in the balance, subject to the least whim of Tiberius's deadly schemes. Caligula and Drusilla relentlessly expanded their sexual repertoire in an atmosphere of fear which added an edge of desperation to their heated incestuous experiments: they knew that they could be snuffed out at any moment, and copulated in a three-year-long frenzy of non-stop lust, almost never leaving their bedroom. But, when Caligula was nineteen years of age,

Tiberius finally came to the reluctant conclusion that, because of his own backfired schemes of murderous overkill, the volatile youth had unexpectedly become the prize contestant to succeed him as emperor, and so he ordered Caligula to join him on Capri, in order to attempt to mould him with his own harsh vision of the Empire and of the pre-eminent value of rampant sexual excess.

By the time that Caligula was shipped out to Capri, the decrepit Tiberius had descended into a state of increasingly senile lust. Newly-discovered inscriptions from the ruins of his palace there record his fondness for participating in a triple anal penetration, and his demand that every inhabitant of the palace had to bow down each morning in subjugation before the majesty of his diseased, blackened sexual organ. At the same time, he kept the Empire under an iron rod, executing any provincial governors who failed to follow his orders to the letter, and restricting the behaviour of the Empire's millions of inhabitants with rigid edicts. He combined lecherous extravagance with grim austerity, and an almost scientific engagement with expanding the limits of the sexual act. For five years, Caligula had to participate incessantly in all of the emperor's spectacular forays into sexual research, which entailed such pioneering work as mile-long chains of buggery, experiments into the moment when orgasm transformed itself into death (many thousands of young male slaves were strangled or decapitated at the precise moment of ejaculation), and the maximum capacity of the anal aperture. Tiberius recorded all of his discoveries in an autobiography which was believed lost until recently; he planned that when his research had been completed, he would compel every inhabitant of the Empire to spend one hundred per cent of their time emulating the experiments he had devised, so that the known world would finally obliterate itself in one great explosive detonation of semen and severed body parts. Witness to mass torture and execution by day and debased in unspeakable orgies by night, Caligula had no option but to wholeheartedly take part in Tiberius's grand schemes, and gradually came to view them as the natural course of events.

He also had to combat his revulsion for Tiberius as the murderer of his family, and to constantly praise and flatter him, although the dour and fast-rotting emperor disdained any idea that he should be worshipped as a god. Tiberius grew tolerant of Caligula and gave him fatherly advice, but it was always limited to the subjects of bestiality, buggery and thrift.

Mercifully, Tiberius was reaching the end of his reign, although he astonished his entourage on several occasions by appearing to expire, before suddenly resuscitating himself and berating those around him for being too quick to think he had perished. Finally though, on 16 March AD 37, he performed this exasperating trick once too often, and one of his own senior bodyguards, a praetorian commander named Macro, lost his temper and throttled the leering emperor with his own sperm-soiled bedsheets. Although Tiberius's last wish had been that one of his most well-endowed slaves should bugger his corpse, nobody prepared to do so could be found, despite considerable financial incentives. For a while, the imperial succession hovered between Caligula and Tiberius's young grandson Gemellus, and a plan was suggested that they should both become joint-emperors. But Macro allied himself with Caligula, and they managed to side-line Gemellus, eventually murdering the youth by taking turns to ram a white-hot poker up his anus. Macro wanted to be the power behind Caligula and to make him a puppet for his own aspirations, and he began to give Caligula overbearing instructions on how he should behave in public, including a prohibition on Caligula committing incest with Drusilla within the public gaze. Although Caligula owed his accession largely to Macro, he had no intention of substituting one bogus father with another, and Macro soon got his come-uppance, ordered to commit suicide with one sneering remark from Caligula: *"tolmai tis didaskein?"* – "Who dares to command me?" Caligula had finally been liberated from the terror of imminent execution which had haunted his early years, and also from his enforced participation on Capri in Tiberius's grandiose displays of sexual deviancy. On 28 March AD 37, Caligula was given absolute imperial power by the Roman

Senate. Now, master of the Empire, he could bugger the entire population of the world if he wanted to.

Caligula soon discovered that Tiberius had been so avaricious and tight-fisted that, over his reign, he had accumulated more money than could be calculated under the Roman numerical system. The coffers of the Empire were bulging, and Caligula set about spending with a vengeance. He won over to him the plebeian scum of Rome by luxuriantly renovating the arena and staging more spectacular gladiatorial combats than they had ever seen. The arena became the primary focus of Rome: its solid-gold, solar anus. Caligula vastly increased the number of games staged in the arena, and made sure that he never neglected to be present for the most prestigious and blood-sodden gladiatorial combats. The massed plebeian hordes remembered Caligula's father, Germanicus, with great affection, and they went into a frenzy of adulatory ecstasy on hearing that Caligula had succeeded the detested Tiberius. They also adored Caligula because he was a visible presence in the filthy backstreets of Rome, often to be seen carried about in a litter with Drusilla by his side, energetically masturbating with one hand while distributing golden coins with the other; the plebeian scum elbowed and crushed one another into the dust in order to simultaneously catch the spurting imperial semen in their mouths and the coins in their hands. They shouted out to Caligula, trying to catch his attention, calling him their "star" and their "little chick".

Another way in which Caligula performed the extra-ordinary feat of totally emptying the imperial coffers in the first year of his reign was by commissioning a mass ritual human and bestial slaughter, to mark his glorious ascension to imperial status: criminals from throughout the Empire were brought to Rome to be massacred in the arenas and temples of the city, their ranks supplemented by innumerable, expendable slaves and by a scattering of attractive citizens who had caught Caligula's eye on his rounds of the city. In all, nearly two hundred thousand animals were also sacrificed; Caligula maintained the vast network of hunters which had been established to collect and transport these animals, in order to provide the arena in the future with a constant supply of lions, bears and other beasts from every corner of the Empire, which were used in the decimation of its dissident elements and other enemies, such as religious cultists and magicians. Already, Caligula considered that he owed it to the adoring plebeian scum to become a god, and the sacrifices at the beginning of his reign formed the first stage in his process of self-deification.

Caligula was also ready to pour away the Empire's wealth into schemes for territorial expansion. The four corners of Caligula's empire stretched from Egypt to Tingitana to the English Channel to the river Rhine: this expanse constituted almost the entirety of the known world, and certainly all of those areas which were viewed by the Romans as being remotely civilized. Beyond the boundaries of the Empire lay the forbidding territories of Britain and Germany, whose inhabitants grouped into morose tribes of ferocious warriors and incessantly pillaged their own dank and forested lands. Even so, Caligula had his eye on the conquest of Britain and Germany: the definitive subjugation of the wild Teutonic hordes had been his father Germanicus's great ambition, and Caligula inherited the desire to extend the territory of the Empire northwards. Since Caligula's own early years had been spent among the dung-reeking encampments of the brutal Roman legions, while his father vainly attempted to subdue the boorish Teutons, he was drawn to the prospect of securing glory for himself by masterminding a final victory over the edge of those northern frontiers. This ambition was coupled with a deep distrust and hatred of the Roman soldiers themselves, since a motley group of them had mutinied when he was a two-year-old child, and had briefly held him hostage in one of the legions' innumerable camps on the Rhine frontier, before the rebellion ended in a bloodbath of retribution. In addition to Britain and Germany, Caligula also had envious designs on the areas beyond the eastern frontier of the Empire, where the fabulously wealthy rulers of weird kingdoms were worshipped as deities by their subjects.

At first, Caligula managed to captivate the aristocratic members of the Senate which nominally governed Rome, as well as the plebeian detritus which swarmed around its streets. Caligula cut a striking figure in his first appearances as emperor before the gathered Senate, which had spent the weeks between Tiberius's death and Caligula's accession in formulating servile tributes to the new emperor. It had fawningly given absolute power to Caligula, thereby effectively annulling itself. Caligula enjoyed making public speeches, especially to such a receptive audience, although his excitable temperament meant that he would quickly become carried away into a gibbering and inarticulate frenzy, spouting saliva in every direction. In his first meetings with the Senate, Caligula made a show of listening to their advice and promising to rule wisely, and he created a favourable impression. The members of the Senate saw before them a tall, heavily built young man of twenty-four, with a strangely elongated forehead that was deeply indented with piercing, manic eyes. From his long years spent perpetually indoors, taking part in Tiberius's sexual experiments on Capri, Caligula's complexion had become intensely pallid; he suffered from chronic insomnia and emanated an aura of restless fatigue, and he always sucked his lower lip under his upper teeth. He appeared ungainly, his hefty torso poised on spindly legs. But, in contrast with the addled and leering figure of the aged Tiberius, who had leaked sexual fluids and booming flatulence with every step, the Senate optimistically viewed Caligula as the epitome of moderation and youthful vigour. The sight of the more-or-less coherent and sentient young Caligula was a relief to them, since at that point, he was expected to reign for the next fifty to sixty years. However, by the end of his reign, under four years later, Caligula would have finalized plans to massacre the entire Senate and destroy its meeting hall, and it was only through an ultimate mischance that the gang of pompous sycophants survived. But for the moment, the senators took turns in delivering grovelling speeches in which every part of Caligula's majestic anatomy was exalted.

Caligula spent the first months of his reign engaged

almost entirely in incestuous copulation with his sister Drusilla. Now that nobody could tell him what to do, he was avid to flaunt his attachment to Drusilla to the maximum degree in public, and a special, miniature amphitheatre was erected where the plebeian scum could, for a small fee, sit and watch their emperor bugger his sister on a stage of solid gold. Drusilla was an active participant in these spectacles, matching her older brother in deviance, and Caligula made it clear that, on the rare occasions when they resorted to vaginal sex, he intended that they would produce a male child, born of rampant incest, who would become the legitimate heir to the Empire. But on most occasions, the crowd would roar with uncontainable ecstasy as Caligula rammed his foot-long rod of imperial *mortadella* into Drusilla's initially resistant, then deeply welcoming anus; simultaneously, Caligula's favourite gladiator, Superbus, from the mountains of eastern Tingitana, would brandish his rigid packet of fourteen-inch *merguez* between both fists and then force it into the emperor's excruciatingly pulsing rectum. Caligula regularly hired well-known professional studs from every corner of the Empire to take part in these public sessions, and also occasionally brought in a few hideously deformed freaks and dwarfs to add a frisson to the proceedings. He enlisted the services of the more well-endowed senators, who were initially delighted to bask in the radiant glare of Caligula's imperial lust. In any case, they had nothing better to do, since now that they had given Caligula absolute power, they had no laws to make and spent all their time discussing what colours the Senate's meeting hall should be redecorated in. Soon, however, the senators had been tired out by the inexorable sessions of copulation, which were interrupted only when Caligula left the sexual amphitheatre to go and watch the gladiatorial atrocities and other blood-sodden massacres in the nearby arena. One of the most well-endowed senators, Valerius Catallus, famously commented that he had been forced to bugger the emperor so often that he had totally worn himself out in doing so. The professional studs, on the other hand, just kept on pumping. Not all of the plebeian scum of Rome approved of Caligula's public incest, and dark mutterings were heard from the city's magicians and oracles that such outrages would bring the wrath of the gods down on the Empire. The magicians employed "curse tablets" – small blocks of lead, smeared with blood and ashes, into which hostile incantations were scratched – against Caligula. The followers of the innumerable clandestine religious cults whispered that the mouth of hell would open up and swallow Caligula into its fiery bowels. Fortunately, Caligula possessed an extensive network of spies and eavesdroppers, and the magicians and cultists invariably found themselves in the arena, minus their heads, thereby bringing a convenient end to their gloomy predictions and vitriolic curses.

After five months of unremitting carnal depravity, Caligula suddenly fell ill, and hovered close to death in a delirious state of fever for nearly four weeks. His doctors feared the worst, and contenders for the succession began to jockey for position, pushing one another out of the way so that they could rip the great imperial ring from Caligula's finger at the moment he expired. Since Caligula had no clear heir, the succession would have to be decided by a violent power struggle. The fever went on, and Caligula's face became covered with streaming orange pustules. The odour of death seeped through the palace. The plebeian detritus gathered at the palace gates, wailing; in the first months of Caligula's reign, they had experienced the most luminescent moment in the entire history of Rome, and feared that it was now to be snatched from them. But Caligula was strong, and he eventually pulled through. On awakening, the first sound he heard was the voice of an obsequious senator declaring that he was ready to give up his own life if Caligula could survive; the emperor immediately took up his offer and ordered him to be killed on the spot. He then demanded a list of all of those who had eagerly anticipated his death, and had them tortured and slaughtered without compunction. Their severed heads were piled up on his bed, where he lay recovering his strength. Then, as soon as he could stand upright, he raided the last treasure chests left over from Tiberius's surplus, and threw seventy thousand golden coins to the rejoicing plebeian masses that had gathered beneath the palace's balconies. After his recovery, Caligula decided that now, he would only ever die when he himself wanted to, and, if it suited him, he would simply not die at all. His self-deification was drawing ever nearer.

Two of Caligula's three sisters had been involved in the unseemly squabbling for power that had gone on while the emperor was in his delirious coma; Drusilla had been the sole sister to have actively hoped for her brother's recovery, and this only deepened Caligula's attachment to her. The guilty sisters, Agrippina and Livilla, were the only conspirators not to be slowly minced and then decapitated; Caligula reflected on his sisters' punishment, and then turned them over to the crowd. He decreed that every member of Rome's plebeian scum, down to the lepers and the freaks, had the right to demand whatever deviant sexual act they desired from the sisters for a period of five days. A special marquee was erected in front of Caligula's palace, and the emperor himself made occasional visits to see how the event was progressing, although he quickly re-established his own rigorous schedule of public incest and buggery, coupled with frequent visits to the gladiatorial arena. An imperial commission stood by the stage where the action was taking place, fully documenting each sexual demand made by the plebeian detritus and the time it took for Caligula's sisters to satisfy it. When the five days were up, Caligula went to the marquee to see his dishevelled but still spirited sisters. He told them that because they had stood up so well to mass copulation on a grand scale (seven thousand deviant sexual acts in one hundred and twenty hours: an impressive average rate of over fifty sex acts per hour), he had indulgently decided to spare their lives; instead, he would exile them to the remote Pontian islands. However, Agrippina was seven months' pregnant at the time, and Caligula permitted her to remain in Rome until after she had given birth, on 15 December AD 37. At first, Caligula mischievously ordered that she had to name the child after his drooling cretin of an uncle, Claudius; but he then relented, and allowed her to choose whatever name she wanted. Agrippina's child would bear the name of one of the few emperors ever to remotely rival Caligula in the sheer intensity of his grandiose and arbitrary slaughter: Nero.

Meanwhile, the Empire was functioning smoothly, except for its rapidly diminishing treasury. Caligula had won over most of Rome's philosophers at the outset of his reign by announcing a regime of total freedom of expression; Tiberius had instigated a policy of rigorous censorship and prohibition on what could be said and published in the Empire. The philosophers were nonplussed, however, when they discovered that they were now expected, on pain of death, to devote their newfound freedom entirely to composing essays and speeches extolling Caligula's libertarian policies: any philosopher who broached another subject would instantly have his hands chopped off and his mouth sewn up. In another liberal move, Caligula freed all of the Empire's political prisoners. But in almost all cases, the prisoners were far too exhausted by years of torture and malnutrition to celebrate their release, and so Caligula then had them immediately re-arrested for the crime of ingratitude; they were transported to Rome, without exception, to serve as fodder for the carnage of the arena. Caligula's innovative policies followed a dual regime of freedom and slaughter, with the latter intractably succeeding the former. In matters of the government of the Empire, Caligula found that he had very little time available to devote to administration, once he had fulfilled his onerous duties to buggery. He therefore conceived a policy in which, whatever problem came up in any part of the Empire, he would take no action whatsoever. He believed that, in every instance, it was better not to interfere, and eventually matters would sort themselves out of their own accord. Because the dour Tiberius had instituted a highly efficient and incorruptible system of administration for the Empire before he decided to dedicate his time to wholesale debauchery on Capri, everything did in fact continue to run smoothly during Caligula's inactive regime. Whenever anxious deputations arrived at the palace from the unruly provinces of the Empire, notably Judea and Egypt, Caligula would smile benignly at the delegates and tell them to enjoy themselves in Rome while he considered their problems; the delegates then invariably became caught up in the furore of the arena or in the public spectacles of copulation, and quickly forgot about whatever matters had seemed so urgent to them when they had first arrived in the city. The Empire continued to operate at full tilt, although Caligula knew that the previously-groaning imperial coffers bequeathed to him by Tiberius were now empty, and he would need to come up with some new wealth-generating schemes before too long.

Overall, the first year of Caligula's reign had been a blistering success: the plebeian scum were in ecstasy at the regime of atrocity and sexual spectacle which their emperor unstintingly provided for them; the Senate now had endless free time to enjoy, and the philosophers had been granted complete liberty of expression. It appeared that Caligula's reign would be the pinnacle of Roman civilization in every field, and that it would continue for many more decades. But then, without warning, everything fell apart. On 10 June AD 38, Drusilla suddenly died, at the age of twenty-three. The doctors diagnosed "a surfeit of buggery". She had just concluded a non-stop twenty-hour session with her brother and seven outrageously well-endowed studs who had recently arrived from the province of western Caesariensis, the conclusion of which had been a near-apocalyptic collective orgasm whose devastating celebro-neural implications had sadly proved terminal for Drusilla. Even after her face turned bright blue and *rigor mortis* set in, Caligula kept on berating the doctors and instructing them to resuscitate his sister. His screams of anguish rang throughout the city. The only solution now was to transform Drusilla into a god; after thoroughly sodomizing his sister's icy body for the final time, Caligula quickly set to work issuing edicts and proclamations. Within a few weeks, every district of Rome had a temple devoted to Drusilla's deification, and statues of the new goddess appeared all over the Empire, from the greatest cities to the smallest hamlets. The human Drusilla now became the god Panthea – a name which indicated that, in her deified splendour, she both encompassed and surpassed all of the other gods.

Although the plebeian scum of Rome were happy to accept that Drusilla was now a god (her deification was marked by a spectacular set of gladiatorial games in the arena), the members of the Senate and the city's philosophers opposed Caligula's edicts, on the grounds that only outstanding emperors, such as Augustus, had the right to become gods. This obstinacy drove Caligula into a psychotic frenzy of unparalleled proportions. The blubbering philosophers had their tongues pulled out, and were then dispatched to the arena to be publicly crucified upside-down while being burnt alive; the recalcitrant senators, too, fell victim to Caligula's near-divine wrath. In front of the emperor's eyes, their executioner slit open each senator's stomach with a skinning knife and then gradually extracted his internal organs with white-hot scissors and pliers, making sure that the removal of the organs occurred in such a sequence that the senator remained aware of what was happening to him for the longest possible duration; then, when a steaming heap of his own reeking internal organs had gathered in full view of the senator's horrified eyes, the executioner was instructed by Caligula to finish him off, by gradually sawing apart the screaming senator's body, until it slumped to the ground in two blood-spurting pieces. Caligula famously ordered the senators' executioners: "Strike so that they may feel that they are dying." And rather than rescinding the posthumous deification of Drusilla, Caligula decided that he himself would soon join her as a deity, and that he would certainly not have to die before it happened.

In the months after Drusilla's death, Caligula journeyed south, to Naples and then Sicily, trying to distract himself. He took with him the cremated ashes of his sister in a tubular golden urn, and would often open up the urn and thrust his imperial weapon into the powdered debris of grey bone shards, desperately trying to resuscitate his sister with his regal semen. But the failure of this strategy only increased his sense of psychotic desolation, and he concluded that it was now time for him to create the foundations for a great dynasty of incest, perversion and slaughter, that would rule the world for many millennia. In deciding on a choice of sexual partner for this magnificent project, Caligula hovered for a while between his favourite horse, Incitatus, and a human contender named Caesonia, who had the reputation of being the most lascivious woman in Rome. In the end, Caligula decided on Caesonia, and after some lengthy sessions of vaginal intercourse (a novelty for Caligula), she soon became pregnant. The emperor compensated the disappointed Incitatus by giving the horse considerable decision-making political power over the entire Empire, as well as by constructing a massive new stable of marble and silver, encrusted with diamonds; he also gave Incitatus a place of honour at all his banquets, and included the horse's name in every sentence he spoke. But Incitatus remained inconsolable. Then, in April AD 39, Caligula married Caesonia, and in the following month she gave birth to a baby girl with a savage temper, whom Caligula naturally named Drusilla. The first stage in his great plan for a lunatic dynasty of incest had come to fruition, although Caligula realised with exasperation that he would now have to wait for a few years before he could inseminate the reincarnated Drusilla and produce a rightful heir for the Empire.

In order to consolidate the glory of his new dynasty, Caligula decided that some unprecedented public spectacles and spectacular military triumphs would be in order. The first of these grandiose events was the spanning of the Bay of Naples, in July AD 39, by a immensely long arc of boats. This intricate feat, known as the "bridge of Baiae", was executed on the emperor's instructions by many thousands of engineers, aided by a multitude of slaves. The bridge, made from commandeered merchant ships that had been bound together in a double line, was paved over with a flat road of marble able to carry the weight of many chariots. Caligula dispatched a gang of grave-robbers to plunder the tomb of Alexander the Great in Egypt, and they brought back the breastplate which Alexander had worn in all of his great victories against Asian despots. The plebeian scum of the whole of southern Italy were herded to the bay, where they cheered in adulation at the appearance of Caligula, wearing the legendary breastplate under a cloak of purple cloth that was embedded with chunks of gold and precious gems. Caligula rode from one end to the other of the bridge as the watching crowd whipped itself into a cacophonous frenzy. On the second day of the spectacle, Caligula drove out on a chariot to the centre of the bridge, followed by a dazzling procession of thousands of his most trusted bodyguards. Caligula had with him the young son of the King of Parthia, who had been captured and brought to Rome as a hostage; the subjugated presence of the tyrant's son served to demonstrate Caligula's ascendancy over all of the bestial Asian hordes which posed a perpetual danger to the Empire's eastern frontier. Caligula climbed onto a splendid platform raised over the bridge and addressed the plebeian masses on the shoreline, praising his own extravagance. Although his speech rapidly degenerated into saliva-spouting incoherence, the entranced millions of plebeian scum barked out their reverence for Caligula's pearls of wisdom. Finally, on the second night, the spectacle ended with a great celebration, illuminated by a series of huge pyres which flamed from the cliffs around the bay, turning night to day. Caligula announced that even the plebeian masses had the right to participate in the alcohol-fired celebration, although when too many of them climbed onto the bridge at the same time, part of it collapsed under their weight and many thousands drowned, elated to their last breath. Undeterred by the fatalities, Caligula began to plan his next great spectacles: the decimation of the brutish Teutonic military forces, to be followed by the conquest of murky Britain.

In early September AD 39, two months after bridging the Bay of Naples, Caligula set out at the head of a colossal army of a quarter of a million soldiers, heading for the city of Mainz on the river Rhine: the centre of all Roman military operations against the Teutonic hordes. Caligula travelled surrounded by a thousand of his elite bodyguards, and the army stretched out for several miles behind them. After the legions, a further army of camp-followers – many thousands of male and female prostitutes, cooks, actors and entertainers of all kinds – followed on. Caesonia and the five-month-old Drusilla, together with a wagonload of well-endowed, attractive slaves exclusively assigned to service the emperor's sexual caprices, also accompanied the vast procession. In all, a travelling city of over half a million people scorched its way northwards, squeezing dry every place it passed through for provisions before leaving it flattened and smouldering. Each night, the legionnaires would gather around immense campfires and sing ominous songs. For the initial stages of the journey, Caligula rode along on horseback, constantly whipping his legions onwards, so that the convoy moved at a breakneck pace. But then, the emperor grew tired of riding and had to be carried by eight sturdy legionnaires, on a litter of swansdown. Throughout the long journey, Caligula amused himself by taking potshots at the dull-witted peasants in the roadside fields, wielding a sort of projectile-shooting bazooka which had been specially designed for him by his engineers. Even from long range, Caligula could nonchalantly take the head off a gormless peasant with one shot. Peasants had a pitifully low rank in the regime of the Roman Empire, which was intended to benefit urban centres and their inhabitants rather than rural workers; peasants figured somewhere between dogs and swine in the priorities of the Empire.

After a journey of forty days, Caligula arrived at the river Rhine. The commanders of the legions stationed there were astounded to see the approaching army, headed by the emperor in person; some of the older legionnaires remembered Caligula from when he had been taken to the Rhine bases as a small child by his father, the ever-popular Germanicus, and they feebly cheered his arrival. The struggle with the Teutonic savages had been going on for many decades already, punctuated by occasional crossings of the Rhine by the legions and ferocious battles with the bearded and godless Teutons, notably the savage Chatti tribe. Exactly thirty years previously, three of the Roman legions had been completely obliterated in the legendary Battle of the Teutoburg Forest, the aftermath of which had seen the entrails of over seventy thousand Roman soldiers hanging from the branches of that dank forest's trees; the boorish Teutons had sliced off and pickled the massacred legionnaires' testicles, and had only finished eating them in the previous year. It was a defeat that still cast a heavy pall over the entire Empire, and Caligula was determined to avenge it. Over the subsequent decades, the brutish Roman legions stationed at the Rhine had grown increasingly mutinous and uncontrollable, while their commanders had almost given up on defeating the untameable Teutonic hordes and had lapsed into weary lassitude and corruption. Caligula ordered the executions of the most inept commanders and made fresh appointments from among his entourage, although the new commanders proved to be just as incompetent as the previous ones. He also gave stirring speeches to the Rhine legions, but they had all been marooned out in those bestial provinces for far too long, and simply stared back at .the gesticulating, saliva-spouting Caligula with vacant expressions. The wild Teutons had heard that the Roman emperor himself was there, and thousands of them gathered on the river's far bank to chant abuse at Caligula and to make obscene gestures.

Caligula was discouraged by the surly behaviour of the near-mutinous legions in that infernal backwater, and was already regretting his decision to launch the campaign; he missed the hysterical adulation which he received in Rome from his plebeian scum, together with the constant supply of atrocity and high-calibre buggery he had access to there. But he was still determined to execute a spectacular triumph against the Teutonic savages that would serve to saturate his reign with glory. Although it was clearly too dangerous for him to stage a battle against the invincible Teutons using only the loyal troops he had brought with him from Rome, he devised an ingenious alternative strategy. Some of his own bodyguards were of German origin, so Caligula arranged for twenty of them to be dressed up in the woolly costumes favoured by the devilish Teutons, and ordered them to hide in a nearby wood; he then raced after them with his army of two hundred and fifty thousand men, and courageously captured them. On returning to the legions' camp, the prisoners swore oaths of allegiance in German to Caligula and debased themselves by kissing his boots, before being summarily slaughtered. News of Caligula's great triumph was urgently sent back to Rome, although the disabused Rhine legions simply rolled their mutinous eyes.

After his magnificent victory on the Rhine, Caligula headed west, arriving at the city of Lyons, in the backward province of Gaul, at the end of October AD 39. He intended to rest for the winter in that relatively-salubrious city, before launching his great invasion of Britain. At this point, the imperial treasury had reached rock-bottom, and Caligula knew that he would have to generate some substantial new funds. The wealthy inhabitants of Lyons were enthralled to have the Roman emperor himself staying in their provincial city, and they had money to burn. Caligula hit upon the brilliant idea of selling his excrement to them for the same price as its weight in gold. The Roman governor of Gaul had been expelled from his palace in Lyons to make room for the emperor, and Caligula spent his first months in the palace engaged in eating enormous portions of *polenta* in order to generate the material that would ensure a maximum revenue (even today, in rural northern Italy, a large portion of *polenta* is called a "Caligula"). He discovered that there was no shortage of takers, and the wealthy, starstruck provincials eagerly lined up outside the palace to make their purchases of his near-divine imperial excrement, which was canned in little brass containers that added to its weight. Soon, the Empire's coffers were starting to bulge again. Caligula realised that the unsophisticated provincials would literally buy anything at all with an imperial aura; to satisfy the demand, he had his exiled sisters' possessions brought to Lyons and personally auctioned them off at a series of public sales. He cajoled the avid buyers, and protested that they were snapping up the imperial possessions at such low prices that it was daylight robbery. When his sisters' possessions had all been bought, Caligula ordered that everything which had belonged to the deceased emperors Tiberius and Augustus should also now be dispatched to Lyons, on a mule train that stretched non-stop between the two cities. The auctions' takings flooded the palace and poured out of the windows; Caligula had to live in one small room, since every other space in the palace was filled up with bloated treasure chests. One evening, while Caligula was gambling with his cronies, he suddenly left the room and ordered that a list be drawn up of the hundred most wealthy families in Gaul; he then commanded that every member of the families should be immediately slaughtered, since if someone died without an heir in the Roman Empire, their entire inheritance passed directly to the emperor himself. He then returned to the gambling table, and taunted his cronies by telling them that while they had been busy gambling for a few pennies, he had just netted a fortune in the space of five minutes. The money poured in. Apart from using some of it to build a monumental statue to his deified sister in the main square of Lyons, Caligula hoarded all of the rest; he had the swollen treasure chests loaded onto wagons and added to his army's convoy. By the first months of AD 40, Caligula had completely bled the city and the whole of Gaul dry, and even the gullible provincials were getting restive and starting to demand their money back; the emperor then abruptly left Lyons with his army, and headed for the coast of the English Channel.

In March AD 40, at Boulogne, Caligula gazed out over the narrow expanse of rough sea towards Britain. The Senate in Rome had already sent him a letter acclaiming him as "Britannicus", the conqueror of Britain, so his imminent victory over the gloomy island was a foregone conclusion. The white cliffs could be made out on the far side, shrouded in mist and thunderclouds, and topped by great lines of gesticulating human figures, brandishing enormous axes; their rumbling curses could be heard even on the Gaul side of the Channel. Caligula then came up with the most ambitious and innovative plan of his entire reign. He decided that his legions should split into two halves and then furiously decimate one another, leaving no survivors whatsoever; this mass carnage would so terrify the Britons that they would immediately surrender their island to Caligula. But, when Caligula excitedly announced his plan in a speech to the massed legions, he discovered to his astonishment that they were unreceptive to their own annihilation. Before long, though, he had formulated an alternative plan, which was just as brilliant. He stood on a specially-erected platform of solid gold and barked out his orders, commanding all of the soldiers to collect as many seashells as they could carry from the beach; once the shells had been gathered into jute sacks, Caligula would take them back to Rome as the spoils of his conquest, with each shell representing an enslaved Briton. He would then return at some nebulous point in the future to actually undertake the mundane business of putting the primitive British hordes into chains and delivering them for slaughter in the Roman arena. The soldiers enthusiastically filled up the sacks, preferring this idea to that of their own collective extinction, and the brimful sacks of shells were added to Caligula's endless baggage train. With his great mission fulfilled, the emperor now ordered his army to form up for their triumphant return to Rome, and they soon headed off, leaving the glowering Britons still hurling black maledictions from their own side of the Channel.

As Caligula approached Rome in May AD 40, the plebeian scum surged out of the city in one delirious throng to welcome him back. He immediately ordered that the greatest games of gladiatorial combat and mass atrocity in the history of Rome be organized to celebrate his magnificent victories. The three-month-long games, in which untold thousands of criminals, magicians and dissidents of every kind would be slaughtered, proved so expensive that they consumed almost the entirety of the money which Caligula had extorted from the citizens of Gaul. But, for Caligula, it was worth it. The plebeian masses pleaded with Caligula not to leave Rome again, since during his absence they had been subjected to numerous restrictions and prohibitions on their behaviour by the Senate, which had been trying to claw back its power. And on his return journey to Rome, the emperor had himself been constantly fulminating against the Senate, since they had committed the grave error of not sending him sufficient congratulations for his unprecedented feats of courage and brilliance beside the English Channel. To add insult to injury, they had dispatched to Gaul his drooling freak of an uncle, Claudius, to deliver their restrained acclaim; the furious Caligula had lifted the slobbering cretin into his arms and thrown him headfirst into a sewer, from which he emerged caked in reeking liquid dung. Now, Caligula was thinking of massacring the entire Senate; he slapped the blade of his imperial sword in the flat of his hand, and yelled in the direction of the Senate's meeting hall: "I'm on my way, and so is this!" On his return journey, he had carefully filled two notebooks with a hit-list of the senators' names, titling one notebook "Sword" and the other "Dagger". He was also planning to use exactly the same murderous income-generating strategies on the wealthy families of Rome which he had successfully employed in Gaul.

But above all, Caligula had decided that it was now time for his own deification. He spent the entire summer of AD 40 in one of his many lavish villas outside Rome, rigorously preparing to be a god. He sent for the most adept magicians from every corner of the Empire, and they spent several weeks in a darkened room with Caligula, revealing every last secret of their art to him. In a final ceremony, they formed a circle around the emperor and, incanting strange invocations in many tongues, they infused his naked body with all of their arcane powers, so that it radiated golden jets of fire from every orifice. After that, Caligula commanded the greatest philosophers of the Empire to assemble at his bedside and impart to him their most hidden and deepest wisdom; this encounter proved less successful, since Caligula was resistant to hearing banalities such as "the spirit and the body are one" being spouted, and he finally grew exasperated and ordered his bodyguards to jam white-hot pokers up the philosophers' anuses. When Caligula heard the philosophers' excruciated screams of terror and agony, he commented: "Now that is true philosophy". Then, he sent for the most sexually dexterous individuals from the remotest reaches of the Empire – members of the Quinquegentanei, Marataocupreni, Cietae, Brisei and Garamantes tribes of wild nomads, who devoted their time entirely to intensive sexual experimentation and had only ever been partially caught in the merciless grip of Rome – to teach him the legendary "seven great secrets of sexual self-annihilation".

Finally, Caligula was ready to become a god. He entered Rome without warning on 31 August AD 40 and headed straight for the arena, where the final day of the games which celebrated his magnificent victories against the Teutonic hordes and the savage Britons was taking place. Under the rapt gaze of his adoring plebeian masses, he waded about in the glistening lake of blood which had collected from the gladiatorial killings and the wholesale slaughter of criminals and cultists, smearing it over his body and drinking it. He then ordered his favourite gladiator, Superbus, to bugger him under the transfixed eyes of one hundred thousand delirious plebeian scum, along with a scattering of disgruntled senators and fearful merchants. A mysterious eight-foot-tall figure, masked and dressed entirely in black, held a scimitar poised over Superbus's head as he pumped away. Then, at exactly the same moment that the gasping Superbus ejaculated and the emperor convulsed in a grandiose orgasm, the black-clad figure skimmed the gladiator's head from his body with one great blow of the scimitar. A spurting torrent of arterial blood fountained up into the air from Superbus's severed neck at the same moment as his terminal semen flooded the emperor's divine rectum, the great gouts of scarlet blood falling on Caligula's head and into his mouth as he twisted around to receive them. The crowd, too, was instantly propelled into a blistering paroxysm of orgasm and elation, and in the celebratory crush, many thousands of the plebeian detritus found themselves being trampled underfoot and killed. The severed head of Superbus rolled across the dirt of the arena, a contented expression on its face from the privilege of having participated in Caligula's deification.

After the ceremony, Caligula was exhausted, and he lay weak and dispirited in his palace for almost a month. He realised that he could never recapture the intense sensory cataclysm of his deification, and that from now on, it would all be downhill for his corporeal existence. A new plan began to form in his head. Meanwhile, great temples for the cult of the new god Caligula were being erected in every district of Rome, as well as in settlements across the entire Empire, from the smallest hamlets to the greatest cities. A magnificent temple was constructed on the Palatine hill in the centre of Rome, and Caligula appointed his corporeal self as the head priest, to revere his deified self; he remembered the loyalty of Incitatus, and made his devoted horse the deputy head priest of the temple, with a generous salary and considerable responsibilities for overseeing the rites to be celebrated there. All over the Empire, in temples dating from earlier eras, the statues of the gods which had previously been worshipped there – often for millennia – were abruptly jettisoned, so that the statue of the god Caligula could stand in their place. This desecration often led to public opposition and uprisings, especially among the religious cultists of Judea and Egypt. In some instances, Caligula was forced to back down, since the unrest grew so virulent that it threatened to erupt into open warfare. The wild-eyed cultists massed in the main squares of their backward towns, spitting out glossolaliac exclamations interspersed with dark maledictions against Caligula's reign. The Roman legions were stretched to the limit, as they mercilessly clubbed the demonstrators and crucified the ringleaders upside-down. Caligula resented the opposition raised to his deification: he especially disliked the idea of being ranked as a secondary deity, subjugated to some bizarre, abomination-wielding god who was supposed to have created the world. In fact, the world – together with the entire cosmos – had emerged from nowhere, as a malevolent accident, and only an intensive regime of unrestrained slaughter and buggery could set that tainted world to rights. Caligula was impatient to meet the other gods and to exert his taboo-busting authority over them.

In October AD 40, Caligula faced the first and only serious opposition to his reign, in the form of an attempted coup led by four seditious senators: a father and son, both named Anicius Cerialis, together with their two co-conspirators,

Betilienus Bassus and Sextus Papinus. The plot had the backing of the legions that Caligula had wanted to decimate at Boulogne, and was certain of success, until it suddenly collapsed at the last minute when the son (who would subsequently be butchered under the reign of Nero) betrayed his father and the entire conspiracy to Caligula, in a fit of sycophantic delirium. The emperor was pleased to hear the obsequious son blurt out his denunciations of his own father, and decided to pardon him. Once the son had thoroughly buggered and throttled his father into oblivion, Caligula rewarded him with the governorship of an obscure province. The other senators, together with the commanders of the mutinous legions, faced more severe penalties: some of them were tortured with fiery prongs until their entire bodies had turned black and smouldering, while others found themselves spiked from end to end, then roasted over an open fire, before being summarily beheaded. So many suspected conspirators were due to be put to death that their overworked executioners had divided them into two separate batches, to be killed on successive days. But, once the slaughter was underway, Caligula grew impatient to see everybody die all at once, and the executioners had to work at a relentlessly high speed in order to butcher all of the conspirators on the same evening. While he watched the executions, Caligula tried on a series of costumes associated with a range of gods: Mars, Hercules, Dionysus, Jupiter, Venus and Juno. He decided that he preferred the costumes of the female gods, and spent the final months of his reign wearing increasingly extravagant women's robes.

Caligula grew more arbitrary in his choice of which Romans should be executed, and took to being driven around the city in a luxurious carriage so that he could spot likely contenders for immediate evisceration. He had developed a particular repulsion for people with foppish hairstyles, and anyone caught committing such a crime against fashion (and against his own balding pate) faced the knife. He also detested having his own distinctive dress sense being encroached upon. When King Ptolemy of Mauretania, an African despot who had allied himself to Rome, unwittingly appeared in the arena wearing an attractive purple robe, Caligula had him executed on the spot, on the grounds that only he himself was allowed to wear that colour. But, even in his most heated excesses, the emperor never turned against the plebeian scum of Rome; when they saw him passing by in his carriage and shouted out affectionate insults at him – calling him an "idiot" or a "whore" – Caligula would simply smile benignly and throw them showers of golden coins, although this magnanimity invariably caused a murderous scramble which would lead to the deaths of the emperor's insulters.

The surviving senators occasionally whispered to one another that Caligula had gone insane, but the example of what had happened to their massacred colleagues meant that they kept quiet about their misgivings in public, and in the presence of the emperor, they ostentatiously praised his costumes and his divine justice. Caligula set up a whorehouse in an annex of the palace, using the senators' wives as common prostitutes who could be hired by even the lowliest freaks, dwarfs and lepers; after Caligula had blissfully rolled around on the profits, they went directly into his still critically-depleted treasure hoard. The riled senators had to reconcile themselves to this outrage, and to settle in for a long haul – despite his ever more deviant and erratic behaviour, Caligula was still young and bursting with health, and clearly had many decades' worth of escalating atrocity and sexual depravity left to undertake. Caesonia, too, knew that her husband had gone deeply berserk, but Caligula had hardly been a model of sober restraint even in the early days of his reign, and so she accepted the situation and made sure that nobody in Caligula's vicinity ever contradicted him. On one occasion, the emperor spent several days locked in a room of his palace, and then emerged to announce that he had just copulated with the Moon. In the arena, a gladiatorial combat he attended was suddenly interrupted by a raging thunderstorm, and the drenched gladiators abandoned their fight under an ominous black sky of lightning bolts; Caligula was incensed, and ordered the god Jupiter himself to descend from the skies into the arena, so that Caligula could challenge him to a duel. When Jupiter failed to appear, the emperor claimed victory by default. From that moment, everyone who appeared before Caligula had to prostrate themselves on the ground before him and to kiss his boots. He was waiting impatiently for the moment when his daughter Drusilla would be old enough for him to sexually institute his divine dynasty of imperial incest.

After his thwarted duel with Jupiter, Caligula began to make regular appearances in the combat zone of the arena, dressed in the costume of his favourite Thracian gladiators. His opponents, although in appearance the fiercest and most malicious of the gladiators, were always armed only with a flimsy wooden dagger, while Caligula himself brandished an enormous, razorsharp sword of glittering steel. The gladiators faced the dilemma of whether or not they should put up any resistance to the emperor's onslaughts against them: if they raised their feeble daggers against Caligula, the plebeian scum would howl with disapproval, and the imperial bodyguards were always primed to disarm and slaughter them; but, if they allowed the emperor to strike, he would unhesitatingly disembowel or decapitate them, and then revolve with his arms in the air, acknowledging the vast crowd's adulation of his hard-fought victory, his face glowing with deified exhilaration. The only solution for a gladiator intent on survival was to prostrate himself before Caligula, asking for his divine mercy; but the emperor would then allow the crowd to adjudicate on whether or not he should cut his opponent's throat, and the plebeian scum had grown increasingly capricious and blood-crazed since Caligula's return from his campaign, in a strange symbiosis which revealed the crowd's deep – and at least partially-reciprocated – attachment to their emperor. In the final months of his reign, Caligula introduced an innovation into the intricate regulations governing gladiatorial combats. From that moment, no gladiator was allowed to blink during his bout in the arena; if he did so, he faced immediate disqualification and the summary confiscation of his eyeballs. The combatants rapidly adapted themselves to the divine edict; a determined gladiator could learn to stare unblinkingly, even when his opponent's sword was descending in an unstoppable trajectory that would slice his skull cleanly in two.

In the final months of AD 40, Caligula grew so exasperated with the surly senators and the provincial opposition to his deification that he suddenly left Rome and travelled to the nearby Lake Nemi, in the Alban hills, where the engineers who had been responsible for bridging the Bay of Naples had built for him a fleet of vast and sumptuous galleys. Each vessel was decorated with a jewelled prow and elaborate mosaic floors, and had marble walls encrusted with solid gold; the galleys also possessed their own central heating system and a supply of running water which fed lavish steam baths. Some of the vessels had been assigned to Caligula's sexual entourage, while Caesonia and Drusilla each had a galley of their own, manned by a crew of over a thousand slaves. The largest and most magnificent vessel had been reserved for Caligula's exclusive use, and at night, he would recline in the open air on a bed of swansdown, and look directly upwards at the stars, in solitude, reflecting on his future. A chorus of eunuchs sang softly to him from an adjacent vessel as he lay there, deep in thought. It was on Lake Nemi that Caligula finally decided that he was tired of the relentless sensory demands of his corporeal existence, and he abandoned his great dynastic scheme, in order to rejoin his deified sister. He regretted having to leave his adoring plebeian masses behind, but he planned to bequeath to them a regime of haywire anarchy and acute urban tumult that would be unrivalled in the history of the world. He consulted with the head of the praetorian guards, the obliging Chaerea, and also began to make plans with the commanders of his imperial bodyguard. Finally, on 10 January AD 41, he staged his ultimate spectacle of degeneracy on the lake: a massive, week-long and non-stop sexual extravaganza in which even the slaves participated, with acrobatic highlights of quadruple buggery that sent screams of ecstasy echoing around the hills. Then, abruptly infuriated with everyone and everything, Caligula ordered that all of the opulent vessels be set ablaze and sunk to the bottom of the lake, with the copulating slaves still obliviously engaged in their headlong sexual frenzy as they drowned. Along with Caesonia and the little Drusilla, Caligula returned to Rome for the last time.

In Rome, Caligula announced an exceptional spectacle of entertainment for his plebeian masses, and an amphitheatre was specially erected for the event. It was a lavish construction, composed of solid silver panels that reflected the rays of the sun in an intense blaze of light; the nails that held the amphitheatre together were made of solid gold. The hybrid building, conceived as both an arena and a theatre, was able to accommodate twenty thousand of the delirious plebeian scum, as well as the surviving senators, for whom attendance was compulsory, on pain of death. Caligula oversaw the construction, and commanded his engineers to spare no expense on a sumptuous altar of gold and precious gems, dedicated to his own deific cult, which was positioned to one side of the space. The entire construction adjoined the gates of the palace, so that Caligula could pass through one of a number of tunnels that led directly into the amphitheatre. By the time that the engineers had finished their extravagant work, only two golden coins remained from the entire imperial booty, and Caligula set those aside to be placed on his eyes at the moment when his redundant corporeal existence would come to an end.

Caligula had instructed the commander of the praetorian guard, Chaerea, to ritually butcher him during his spectacle, while Caligula's own bodyguards would massacre all of the surviving senators and then set fire to their meeting hall. With the burden of his sex-wracked body gone, Caligula would then be entirely transformed into an immortal god, and, together with Drusilla, he would continue to rule over the Empire, under the banner of divine buggery, exacting ever-greater sensory infernos of torture, slaughter and incestuous copulation upon the peoples of the known world. Caligula knew that the only surviving candidate for the position of emperor was his cretinous and incapable uncle, Claudius. With the Senate out of the way, total uproar would govern the Empire, and the plebeian scum would run wild in ferocious waves of mass obliteration, careering purposelessly from one end of the imperial domain to the other, in gangs of millions of roaring human figures, leaving scorched and blackened earth wherever they went. With his brilliant plan for the future fully formulated, Caligula then spent several days resting in his palace, in anticipation of the upheavals to come.

On the morning of Caligula's final spectacle, 24 January AD 41, the plebeian masses seethed around the amphitheatre, impatient to be admitted. It was now traditional for them to storm the entrance gates to the Roman amphitheatres in a mad crush as soon as they were opened, leaving many thousands of people dead; the death toll was exacerbated on this occasion by the limited number of overeager scum who could be allowed inside the amphitheatre, which was much smaller than Caligula's grand gladiatorial arena. The crowd settled on the high tiers and waited for the spectacle to begin. Below them, the scattering of surviving senators sat lugubriously. Many of the city's wealthy merchants had by this time been assigned for summary execution (along with their entire families), in order that Caligula could seize their assets, but those who had not yet been earmarked for murder sat in wary silence between the senators and the plebeian scum. Caligula's incontinent moron of an uncle, the drooling Claudius, also joined the crowd. At ground level, the altar of gold and gems glittered in the sunlight, and a performance stage, covered in pristine white cloth, had been set up in the centre of the space. Then, through one of the tunnels that led from the palace, Caligula appeared in a robe of scarlet, flanked on either side by Caesonia and the little Drusilla. He took his place on a diamond-encrusted throne, appearing subdued and preoccupied, and the spectacle began. At a signal from Chaerea, the emperor's glowering bodyguards surrounded the senators, to ensure that not one of them could escape. Caligula's final night on earth had been a troubled one: as usual, he had been tormented by insomnia, and had screamed at the sky, ordering the dawn to arrive. When he did finally fall asleep, he dreamed that he had arrived in the celestial domain of the gods, but Jupiter abruptly kicked him out again, so that he fell back to earth.

To start off the day's entertainment, Caligula came forward with an emerald-studded dagger and slaughtered a flamingo; the blood of the writhing bird spurted in all directions, onto Caligula and the senators in the front tiers of the amphitheatre. Since Caligula was wearing a scarlet robe, the thick blood coating him remained invisible. It was the first time that a flamingo had ever been seen in Rome, and Caligula had wanted to provide astounding innovations to the engrossed crowd right up to the last moment. But the main attraction of the spectacle was to be a dance performance designed by Caligula himself, *Cinyras*, about the epic acts of a heroic figure, consumed with obsessions of incest, who is finally betrayed and brutally murdered, along with his daughter, in a tidal wave of blood. The young Asian dancers who appeared in the performance had travelled specially from the eastern frontier of the Empire. Although the plebeian scum appreciated the denouement of the performance, they found much of it tiresome, and whistled and snorted impatiently, much to Caligula's exasperation. He began to wonder if the plebeian scum deserved what he had in store for them, after all. The second part of the entertainment consisted of another dance performance, *Laureolus*, which again terminated in violence, with the contorted dancers vomiting blood all over the stage, so that by the end of the two performances, the white cloth that covered the stage had been entirely saturated in floods and clots of gore. Most of the dancers had lost their lives during the spectacle, although the three who had performed the roles of the slaughterers had survived, and stood with bowed heads among the heaped-up carcasses of their fellow performers. The crowd initially voiced their approval of the spectacle languidly, but once they spotted Caligula himself vigorously applauding, the acclaim for the entertainment built to a shattering cacophony that lacerated the very air, and the emperor was satisfied with their response. While a group of assistants carried the moribund and blood-sodden performers off the stage by their arms and legs, the surviving performers made their exit via one of the tunnels that led out of the amphitheatre at ground level. Caligula followed the dancers into the tunnel to congratulate them on their performance, and took the opportunity to commit his ultimate act of buggery, servicing the two male and one female dancers in rapid succession. Just before he ejaculated for the last time, he pulled his pulsing imperial pole out of the performer's anus and stepped back into the amphitheatre, under the gaze of the avid plebeian masses, spouting great gouts of divine semen up into the air in elegant arcs, before they fell to the ground and seeped into the dirt. For the first time that day, the crowd now grew acutely excited, sensing that the emperor had prepared an astonishing spectacle for them that would excoriate their transfixed retinas. Caligula made an obscene gesture to Chaerea, and spoke his final word: "Testicles!" The signal for the last act of Caligula's reign had been given.

Chaerea, backed by a brutish squad of ten guards, advanced on the emperor, who was looking blissfully upwards, anticipating his reunion with his deified sister. The crowd expelled a gaping exhalation of horror as their ecstasy instantly turned to sensory acid. The first blow of Chaerea's massive sword came down between Caligula's neck and left shoulder, carving a seven-inch chasm into his entire upper body. The assassin then gratingly extracted his sword in order to strike again, and a cascade of arterial blood shot ten feet into the air. Caligula staggered in agony, but remained on his feet, looking around at the endless tiers of openmouthed, stunned spectators as his vision began to cloud. The grunting Chaerea, who was enjoying his good day's work of deicide, now drove the sword into Caligula's stomach, twisting the blade as it impaled the emperor's intestines and pushed its way through, the tip appearing from his back with a liquid hiss. Once again, Chaerea pulled the sword back out again in a twisting motion, and as it emerged from the gaping hole in the emperor's navel, a large percentage of his intestines exited with it. They fell to the ground in a reeking, slippery heap, still attached to the organs that remained in Caligula's body. Chaerea looked momentarily at Caligula to check whether he wanted the final blow to be struck, and from deep inside the black pall of agony that was falling over his short-circuiting neuro-cerebral system, the emperor's eyes flickered affirmatively at his assassin.

Chaerea rapidly took a step backwards and swung his sword around his head, then lopped off Caligula's head with one precision-aimed blow. The crowd watched in utter dismay as Caligula's head sailed through the air and landed directly on the altar that had been raised to his deification. The lips still moved convulsively, mouthing obscenities, for the fifteen seconds that it took for the blood flow to the brain to gradually extinguish itself. His glaring eyes scanned the awestruck plebeian masses, then a screen of oblivion crossed over them, and, still open, they suddenly dulled. Meanwhile, the rest of Caligula's demolished body began to crumble, and the spindly legs of the imperial carcass clumsily buckled: ferocious scarlet jets began spouting into the air, drenching the spectators in the lower tiers of the amphitheatre, as the wildly spasming heart desperately tried to pump blood towards the now-detached brain. Abruptly, it gave up the futile effort, shutting down the emperor's vastly over-abused sensory network after one final cardiac paroxysm. In a messy tangle of arms and legs, Caligula's body slumped to the ground with a muffled crash, and lay still, on its back. Each of the ten guards who had advanced on the emperor with Chaerea now stepped forward, and simultaneously plunged their swords through the body, pinioning it to the ground. One of the blows sliced through Caligula's well-worn sexual organs, pulping them instantaneously. The reign of the third Julio-Claudian emperor was over.

For a minute, everyone in the amphitheatre looked on in silent stupefaction, at the decapitated and steaming body of the former emperor sprawled alongside the performance stage, and his severed head resting upright in a spreading pool of blood on the altar. The Roman Empire now appeared poised on the precipice of many millennia of uncontrollable uproar and anarchy that would engulf the entire known world. Only Chaerea appeared nonchalant, his task for the day accomplished; using Caligula's perforated robes, he wiped away the blood from his sword and put it back into its sheath. Then, as the imperial bodyguards began to murderously close in on the terrified senators, an authoritarian voice commanded them to stop: Caligula's drooling cretin of an uncle, Claudius, had emerged from the crowd and was standing before the altar. To the amazement of everyone, Claudius barked out a string of orders, bringing all of the guards rigidly to attention. Slowly, it dawned on the crowd that Claudius was no moron after all; he pulled out a sachet of artificial drool from his mouth, and flung it to the ground. The plebeian scum, cowed, filed silently out of the amphitheatre; the relieved senators congratulated one another on their narrow escape from annihilation, and started rushing towards Claudius to pledge their undying allegiance to him.

For Claudius – the sole adult male survivor of the decimated Julio-Claudian family – there had been only one way to survive the murderous onslaughts of Tiberius and then Caligula: by appearing to be an inoffensive, zero-witted fool that nobody could ever be bothered to devote a few moments to slaughtering. His strategy had succeeded. Now, as he soon made clear, he controlled the entire Empire.

Claudius's seizure of imperial power had been completed by the evening. He quickly won over the potentially-mutinous legions by distributing his entire personal fortune among them, and by promising them that he would immediately start planning the glorious invasion of Britain – and this time, the legions would actually cross the Channel, and eventually subdue the boorish British hordes. The remaining members of the Senate had their full powers and privileges restored to them, and responded with obsequious loyalty. The nonplussed Chaerea was instantly taken away and executed for the imperial assassination, and all of the guards who had known of Caligula's grand scheme found themselves being slowly garrotted in the palace's dungeons. Caesonia was tracked down in the palace and mercilessly eliminated; the little Drusilla was swung around by her ankles in the air, until her skull hit the palace wall and her brains spilled out in an elongated exclamation mark of blood and mashed cerebral tissue. Claudius arranged for the body of his predecessor to be partially cremated under cover of darkness, and the ashes buried in a remote location; after Caligula's sisters had been allowed to return from exile, they dug up the decayed scraps of flesh and charred bones, urinated on them, and then fed them to dogs. The pompous senators publicly condemned Caligula's acts of atrocity, and consigned him to perpetual damnation; the temples and statues devoted to his deification were all destroyed, and a profound oblivion fell on his reign (although the memory of it would burst vividly into life again within a few years).

Claudius then faced his hardest challenge: that of winning over the plebeian scum. Once the imperial coffers had been replenished by legitimate means, he ordered lavish games to be arranged. Then, in the most brutal games ever to cast their shadow of infamy upon the Roman Empire, Claudius astounded the crowd by brazenly eating his dinner just as the most blood-sodden killing was taking place; he loudly smacked his lips and beamed at the crowd as he pushed slabs of meat into his gluttonous maw. Throughout the entire games, he never once gave a thumbs-up signal to the defeated gladiators who looked to him for mercy, and he ordered that, at the moment of their deaths, all of the gladiators had to remove their helmets, so that the crowd could watch death at work. Great illuminated screens were erected around the top tiers of the arena, extolling Claudius's magnanimity and detailing the amount of low-value coins which each member of the audience would receive if they co-operated with the new regime. By the end of the games, the plebeian scum were roaring Claudius's revered name. The momentarily divine Caligula had vanished into the endlessly blowing winds that crossed the vast domain of the Roman Empire.

CHAPTER TWO
GLADIATOR:
BLOOD, SEMEN, ECSTASY

The gladiatorial arena was a site both of momentary, intensive freedom and of always-imminent atrocity. Life for its battling participants and entranced spectators began and ended there. The origins of gladiatorial combat had emerged in ritualistic ceremonies designed to placate monstrous deities which were believed to inhabit the borders of the Mediterranean ocean, occasionally insurging into the cities, driven to ferocity by the lack of human sacrifices made to them, in order to wreak turmoil and to swallow entire populations alive. Countless human sacrifices, especially of virgins, infants and pregnant women, were devoted to appeasing those maleficent deities; but the monsters demanded an ever greater deluge of blood. The gladiatorial battles were conceived as a means of avoiding mass human sacrifices, by giving a small group of fearless men the mission of courageously fighting to the death on sacred sites where the monstrous gods would be watching. The intention was that those threatening deities would be awed into a pacified state by the intensive butchery exacted on one another by the extraordinary band of combatants. The gladiatorial fights thus began as a means both to challenge and to give a spectacular performance for the gods, whose great malediction against human life coincided with the very origins of Roman civilization, and would ultimately decimate it.

But by the era of Caligula, those origins had become perverted to a maximal degree. The gladiatorial combats retained their aura of being majestic feats, performed within a hanging pall of blood for the edification of feverishly watching eyes, but their audience was now composed of a hundred thousand human beings, ranging from the most destitute and depraved scum of Roman society to the emperor himself. Necessarily, that emperor took the place of the original deities. Those gruesome, intangible presences crystallized into the unique physical form of the divine emperor himself, who watched the games with a permanent erection, deciding on the life or death of the combatants with a capricious twist of the thumb.

The status of the gladiators had transformed over centuries from that of heroic saviours to that of the most undignified, reviled detritus of the Empire. Whether they were free men or slaves, the gladiators comprised the most disinherited layer of Roman society. Only those few gladiators who became the subject of the crowd's adulation achieved a soaring ascent of their social status, and that lasted only for as long as they were held within the crowd's fickle esteem. In Rome, the gladiators were housed in austere barracks, invariably run by a brutish, aged taskmaster who had himself been a mediocre gladiator (the most eminent gladiators always fought bout after bout until they were themselves slaughtered) who harangued them with nostalgic accounts of how his own era had been better than theirs. Some of the gladiators belonged to the emperor as his personal property, and were trained in schools funded by one of his wealthy acolytes. The gladiators slept on wooden benches in the unheated barracks, and were awakened at four o'clock each morning by having buckets of icy water thrown over them. Since most gladiators only fought two or three brief bouts each year (so that their appearances could be eagerly anticipated for months beforehand by the crowd), they had considerable time on their hands. Once the basic strategies of combat had been learned, over a gruelling induction period of a year to eighteen months, the gladiators were left to their own devices for most of each day, apart from the practice sessions which took place at dawn.

The gladiators were hard men of destitute origin, whose

days revolved around an endless struggle against fear. But noble buggery was the order of the night, and if two combatants from the same school were due to face one another in the arena on the following day, they would invariably spend the preceding night in grunting tussles, to discover who could take the upper hand sexually. As potent symbols of virility – whose sweat was collected and sold as an aphrodisiac – the gladiators were also surrounded by an entourage of female prostitutes and fans, the so-called "screaming whores", who hung around the entrance to the barracks until one or two of them at a time were allowed inside for sessions of multiple penetration. The gladiators evolved a language all of their own, comprising only forty to fifty one-syllable words, accentuated by a system of dismissive grunts and obscene gestures. As a result, on the rare occasions when the gladiators emerged from their barracks, they would find themselves unable to make themselves understood in the streets by the populace, who assumed (often correctly) that they were being propositioned to take part in bizarre sex acts. The gladiators' regime was akin to that of sumo wrestlers in contemporary Japan, themselves similarly sexually idolized and subject to sudden falls from grace; the key difference was that the sumo wrestler's most undignified fate was to be abruptly upended by his opponent into the crowd, whereas the gladiator could very well find himself in the process of being eviscerated alive under the gloating eyes of one hundred thousand dementedly roaring spectators.

The immense amphitheatre which formed the arena for gladiatorial combats during the era of Caligula had been constructed by a wealthy enthusiast, Statilius Taurus, and had already been in use for around thirty years. It would later be destroyed during the reign of Nero, and the Colosseum constructed by Jewish prisoners near its ruins. And Caligula's arena had itself been preceded by innumerable others, accumulating in size and majesty over centuries, each successively replaced when the braying crowd overspilled its limits, or else simply tore it apart in the insane frenzies of bloodlust and aberrance with which the population of Rome was intermittently infected. The arena was built for the mass hordes, and for no-one else. All behaviour was permitted on its upper tiers, where the plebeian scum amassed, crammed together in their thousands. On the lower seating tiers, senators, merchants and wealthy visitors to Rome sprawled on more spacious seating, their attention often diverted to vitriolic in-fighting and score-settling among themselves. In between the rich and the scum, a scattered array of philosophers, magicians and dissidents sat under the close gaze of the imperial bodyguards, since they could be a source of potential trouble. The philosophers often dissimulated their excitement at witnessing the combats by affecting an air of disdain, discussing the futility of life with their companions, while the magicians spent their time prophesying the utter annihilation which would be Rome's due fate.

Poised above the infinitely extending mass of screaming, hooting and overheated bodies, in an enclosed and luxuriant area which gave him the best view of the massacres, the emperor himself could be seen watching the games. It was the emperor alone who had the authority to decide the dates and programmes for the games; an emperor such as Caligula who could be observed relishing every moment – entranced by each beheading, mauling and disembowelment – won the immediate adulation of the crowd. All emperors knew that the most effective pacification of the otherwise rebellious and unruly plebeian scum could be achieved via the most visually spectacular and technologically sophisticated games, with the maximum number of blood-drenched fatalities. The arena became stage to a form of primaeval snuff theatre, a controlled catharsis of unalloyed carnage where the shrieks of the butchered were countered by antistrophes of sexual ecstasy from the onlookers. The importance of ensuring that the games were staged lavishly and regularly was paramount; games could be scheduled to coincide with particular festivals or to mark the anniversary of great events and military victories in the history of the Empire, but could equally well be concocted whenever the plebeian mob showed signs of unrest, or simply when the emperor's deviant whim dictated that they should be held.

The arena was the one place where the lowliest human detritus of Rome could make their voice heard by the emperor. And, if his favourite gladiators were winning and if he was feeling sexually satiated, the emperor could indulge even the most obtuse demands or comments. Short intervals in the combats were assigned for these public interviews between the emperor and his subjects. One by one, a few of the spectators would cautiously get to their feet and yell their contribution out over the echoing arena towards the recumbent emperor. Many emperors liked nothing better than to exchange inane quips with the most mentally damaged of their subjects, in order to show themselves off in the most favourable light. And every emperor – except Tiberius – welcomed ribald repartee of any kind: the more obscene, the better. Mild insults about their inbred physical peculiarities could be levelled at the emperors by the assembled scum (themselves habitually deformed, mentally abnormal and freakish) at such moments, and taken in good heart by even the most murderous tyrants. However, all emperors without exception were notably unreceptive to appeals for particular monetary levies to be lifted, especially if the income from such financial burdens on their subjects could be channelled directly into the capacious imperial coffers. Both Caligula and Nero would unhesitatingly order the slaughter of the hapless person making such an outrageous request, together with the several hundred people sitting around him, who had been contaminated by association. The order would be carried out instantly by the sword-wielding imperial bodyguards, and a mass stampede towards the arena's labyrinthine exits would invariably entail the further deaths of several thousand crushed individuals.

The dates of major gladiatorial combats, each usually lasting for one to two weeks, were announced by erecting notices on tombstones in all of the cities, towns and villages of the Empire. Although most provincial places had their own minor arena and games, the spectacular events staged in Rome itself, under the divine gaze of the emperor, possessed an irresistible attraction. From all over the Empire – from Gortyn in the south to Vetera in the north – the peasants would abandon their animals and crops, the merchants would neglect their business affairs, and the prostitutes would discard their clients in mid-fellatio, and set out in a mass convergence upon the capital. Gangs of brigands would often waylay the would-be spectators as they passed through wild areas, leaving them messily garrotted and hanging from trees, their purses emptied. When the surviving travellers finally approached Rome, often after a journey of many months, the massively over-populated city threw out towards them a sensory tidal wave of raw exhilaration mixed with human and bestial stenches. The wastelands around the arena became saturated with improvised tents, although many spectators simply slept exposed in the open air. The native inhabitants of Rome fleeced and robbed the great influx of visitors, and the intricate tariffs of prostitution (a triple penetration topped the list) soared. Since the entrance to the games was always by free admission, the moment when the arena's gates were opened at dawn proved acutely dangerous, since a swarm of seventy to one hundred thousand crushed-together bodies would try to enter all at once; this was another source of mass fatalities through suffocation. Although a separation between the male and female spectators on the upper tiers of the arena was ostensibly prescribed, it was never enforced. Once the audience was seated, the games would begin immediately – with some summary executions of criminals, purely to whet the crowd's appetite for the far more entrenched combats to come – and would continue, with short breaks every few hours, until the fall of darkness.

No spectator ever left the place they had seized on the tiers: if they needed to urinate or defecate, they would do it on the spot. The human bodies were packed together so closely (often seated on rough wooden benches, although in provincial arenas it was customary to sit directly on the stone tiers) that, as the day went on, huge clouds of steam would rise up from that corporeal overload, and the arena would appear as a heated human cauldron. The vocal noise was unbearably loud, sustained even during the intervals when no conflict or killing was taking place, since the crowd would utilize those moments for acrimonious disputes about the ranking of particular gladiators: such disputes were often resolved only by knife-thrusts discreetly exchanged between the quarrelling factions. At the fall of dark, when the emperor departed and the games concluded for the day, the crowd would reluctantly file out of the arena. Nothing held any importance for them except the next day's continuation of the spectacle, and so they would usually throw themselves to the ground, as close to the arena's entrance as possible, and try to sleep for a few hours, their ears still ringing with a ferocious noise of screams and taunts, mixed with the echoing cries of the maimed combatants.

In the arena, the intricate regime of atrocity at ground level was mirrored by the differing layers of sexual activity underway among the spectators, as the tiers of seating ascended upwards, from the elite of Roman society to its ultimate dross. The preferred sexual act among the aristocracy was invariably fellatio, and the young male and female companions of the elderly senators and merchants were selected for their expertise and subtlety: those sex acts took place almost invisibly, with hands and mouths working in stealthy gestures, all the more sophisticated for their covert nature. But up on the highest tiers of the arena, such delicacy was unnecessary, and the crowds emanated a relentless cacophony of sexual exclamations and neural furore. In the domain of heterosexual acts, the preferred position was with the young woman crouched over the sitting man, both of them facing out towards the struggles in the arena as the woman moved on the man's penis in a rhythm designed to exactly match the rhythms of the combat below – slow and wary at first, and then increasingly frenzied. Often, when a revered gladiator executed a particularly expert sword-thrust, the woman would open her robe as a mark of adulation, revealing the hard-nippled expanse of her breasts and the penis moving in and out of her vagina. The man would be gasping over the back of her shoulder, trying to maintain a clear view on the action below as the woman's spasmodic movements became ever more erratic. But buggery too was a preferred medium of sexual exchange on those high tiers of the arena, both for homosexual and heterosexual participants, and also for those to whom the division between the two sexes evanesced in a miasma of lust and momentary freedom. The same, crouched posture was often adopted; but an equally attractive alternative would be for one participant to kneel on the benches, with a perfect view on the carnage far below, while the other participant stood behind, his penis incessantly grating its way into his lover's rectum. Obviously, this variant would often cause friction within the saturated ranks of the other spectators, since it would block the view of those seated in the rows behind the copulating pairs. The best solution was for those who preferred that sexual position to monopolize the benches at the very top of the arena; as a result, the highest summit of the amphitheatre was crowned with a circle of wild sodomites, whose screams of ecstasy or torn anal muscles gave an urgent texture to the more generalized sound of vaginal penetration and its resulting cries. But many of those cries were, in any event, drowned out in the thunderous bloodlust commotion of the rampant crowd.

The expert capacity of the sexual participants to regulate their acts in intimate tandem with the gladiatorial combats in the arena below was a matter of considerable pride, both for the wealthy denizens of the lower tiers and the plebeian scum of the upper tiers. The crucial factor in that proximity of bloodshed and ejaculation was engrained training and practice – all of the participants demanded a finesse of timing in their couplings. Such expertise sometimes brought great wealth to skilled participants, such as those youthful prostitutes servicing the rich merchants who were able to make their client's semen shoot in a great rush into the air (or into their mouths, depending on the employer's preference) at the exact moment that the struggle below also achieved its resolution. The young girls and boys, able to modulate their buccal pressure with the maximum proficiency, had been intensively schooled, under the tuition of retired prostitutes known as "fuck-masters"; exceptionally well-endowed slaves were strapped down and compelled to undergo bouts of fellatio often extending over twelve to fourteen hours, until their members were so chafed and sore that they would plead to be re-assigned to latrine-cleaning duties. On the upper tiers, such sexual erudition was absent, but a high degree of co-ordination was still achieved, between the moment of orgasm and the moment when the gladiatorial combat ended in the extinguishment or capitulation of one or other of the parties. The eyes of the spectators shifted incessantly between the combat below and the facial contractions and exhaling mouths of their lovers. All sex acts were strictly suspended for the periods when the crowd awaited the raised or lowered thumb of the emperor, even when ejaculation or orgasm were imminent. Then, amid the roaring celebration or dissent which accompanied the emperor's caprice, a flood of multiple ejaculations would immediately convulse the crowd.

The pre-eminent aberrations of the crowd would sometimes result in such a rigorous doubling of carnage and orgasm proving impractical. Carried away by the elation of the arena's atmosphere or by the victory of a favoured gladiator, great chains of copulating figures would amass on the highest tiers. Although three, four or even five spectators could, with much practice, seat themselves on each another's laps, gripping one another by the shoulders and anchoring themselves via their sexual organs, that precarious, tower-like configuration presented the danger of the figures suddenly toppling over at the moment of orgasm; the sheer slopes of the arena meant that a fatal fall could result from such an over-balancing. The more usual arrangement would be to cordon off a rear bench and allocate it exclusively to multiple sexual constellations. A special problem would arise if a spectator had brought a dog or other large animal along to the games (after all, everyone and everything was entitled to free admission), since sexual combinations of human and bestial figures proved to be volatile arrangements: a dog with a penis lodged in its anus and its own penis moving at speed in a vagina would not necessarily be sufficiently attentive to the nuances of the gladiatorial conflict below, and would fire off its semen at inopportune moments.

But, on the whole, the sexual regime of the arena's tiers took its cues from those of the combat below, and the endless waves of acclamation which accompanied the slicing of a defeated gladiator's throat were always mixed with the guttural and ecstatic cries springing from the accomplishment of innumerable sex acts.

The spouting trajectories of blood which punctuated and concluded the gladiatorial combats also had their close counterparts within the crowd. Strategies of power and revenge were at work here. Even the most senior senator would sometimes find his dignity had been ruffled by the spattering impact of a rain of semen onto his bald pate, launched from somewhere further back in the near-perpendicular seating tiers. The crowd watched both for the moment when a stream of rich arterial blood would issue from a wound pierced in a gladiator's flesh, and also for the simultaneous gush of sperm from those in their more immediate proximity. A skilled prostitute, highly trained in the art of fellatio, could direct the geyser of an ejaculating penis towards the head of one of his or her employer's enemies; a direct hit would always be rewarded with a generous payment. Nothing pleased a senator or merchant more than to see his rival or enemy turn towards him, his concentration on the games broken, and glare upwards as the trails of semen dripped down from his apoplectic forehead, trying to search out its source. But for the purists, such as the dour philosophers, such worldly or score-settling uses of ejaculation were perceived as deeply undignified, and they would simply shoot their semen as far into the air as possible, as a gesture encapsulating the futility of all earthly ambitions. Sadly, the high barriers which surrounded the ground level of the arena – ostensibly erected to prevent the wild animals used in bestial combats from leaping among the spectators – prevented the crowd from ever covering the gladiators themselves (either in derision or in adulation) with the tribute of their semen.

One particular sexual spectacle of the arena was reserved only for exceptional occasions. This coincided with those extravagant events designed by the more exorbitant emperors,

Caligula among them, which involved flooding the ground level of the arena through a network of water channels, in order to stage simulations of great naval battles. Immense ships would enter the arena and lock together in conflict; the participants often drowned in the seething water or were obliterated by broadside attacks. Invariably, the engulfing of the arena in water comprised only a small segment of the day's entertainment; the rapid system of drainage enabled the ground to be once again dry and pristine for the next feature of the programme. Such floods naturally required an appropriate reaction from the arena's spectators, and co-ordinated ejaculations were the order of the day. At the climax of the sea-battles – when one faction had bloodily triumphed, and the simulacrum of the ocean had served its purpose and was about to be drained – a collective gush of semen would signal the crowd's appreciation of the emperor's spectacular benevolence. Even those in the crowd without the luxury of a facilitating prostitute or sexual partner were expected to include themselves in that fluidic outburst. They would unleash fountains of urine at that moment of mass ejaculation, so that a gathering wall of semen and urine would descend, in monsoon-like showers, from the top to the bottom of the arena's levels.

At the end of each day's games, it would fall to the slaves assigned to the cleaning of the arena to mop up the accumulated semen and urine from the seating tiers. Just as the gladiators left a morass of blood and rawly severed body parts at ground level, the spectators too had their own duty to imprint the stone of the arena with their corporeal deposits. It was a difficult and dangerous job to prepare the seating for the next day's crowd, and the cleaners would often slip on the treacherous surface and plummet to oblivion from the highest tiers of the arena, where the residue of semen was at its most dense. The cleaners would discover the left-behind corpses of open-eyed spectators, especially those elderly figures whose orgasmic tumult – often undergone beneath a relentlessly burning sky, shaded only by an overhead canopy which was shifted by sailors during the course of the day and offered the dross of the crowd little protection –

had led to cardiac arrest and a swift death. The last echoes of the crowd's screams still hung in the darkening evening air, as the hundreds of slaves worked to channel the sperm and other debris out through stone channels, allowing it to course through a complex of specially-designed chutes, until it was finally ejected from the arena and landed in the dust of the wastelands that surrounded the magnificent amphitheatre, often drenching the people who had camped there.

Every emperor knew that he must himself be seen masturbating during the games, or being assiduously serviced by the Empire's most skilled prostitutes, in order to win the maximum acclaim from the crowd. Caligula, who was renowned for the size of his organ, was always ready to unveil it before the crowd, which responded with gasps of incredulity and adoration. It proved to be a key factor in Caligula's great popularity with the plebeian population of Rome, from the most abject scum upwards. Everyone remembered that Julius Caesar had refused to unsheathe his penis before the crowd, preferring to affect disdain for the sexual spectacle of the arena by reading dull administrative documents during the games. And the emperor Tiberius had been of such a terminally dour disposition that he had refused to even attend the games at all. Those figures were remembered with little affection, as having created nothing of the essential civilization of Rome and as having provided little entertainment for the edification of its voraciously demanding citizens. Caligula, of all the Roman emperors, best understood the fragility of the membrane that separated death and sex, just as he also perceived the ephemerality of the division between anal and vaginal sexual muscles. The arena exacted great sacrifices from everyone who entered it, and most of all from the emperor himself. To wholly fulfil the vital art of sex and death, the corporeally living god Caligula was finally ready to die in order to accommodate the ultimate desire of his expectant subjects, and did so, provoking a sensory seism which came to mark the supreme moment of Rome's perverse history and aberrant civilization.

The entrance of the gladiators provoked the greatest

neurally-detonating rush of noise and sexual energy. Below the surface level of the arena, the gladiators began to make their way through the labyrinthine tunnels which criss-crossed its subterranean vaults. Along the way, they passed by the cages of the wild beasts that would appear later on in the day's entertainment. The lions and panthers roared and lashed out with their razored paws at the gladiators' legs. The floors of their cages were equipped with pulley devices to ensure that they could be suddenly levitated into the arena and catapulted into the open air without any bystanders suffering injury. The very foundations of the arena shook in great spasms as the crowd stamped its two hundred thousand sandaled or bare feet in unison, impatient to see the first gladiator appear for the day's combat. Next, the gladiators passed by the cages assigned for the detrital human elements who would be massacred during that day's games: a miserable collection of sobbing or cursing figures jammed the cages. The most fierce of them were the heavily bearded, sneering prisoners who had been captured during the perpetual battles waged by the Roman legions against the Teutonic hordes along the banks of the river Rhine. Still wearing their woolly costumes, their grim faces scarred by decades of brutish fighting, the unsubduable Teutonic prisoners spat and hurled invective at the passing gladiators as they awaited their own bloody demise. Finally, the gladiators passed the cages which held the condemned members of the many religious cults which proliferated in the Empire, especially in the region of Judea. The naked and dung-smeared acolytes of magicians and dubious prophets lacked the ferocity of the Teutonic captives, and many of them simply huddled together and whimpered in terror at their imminent evisceration; others, still imbued with psychotic fervour, screamed abuse at the gladiators and warned them that their participation in the ungodly regime of Rome would exclude them from one eden or another.

But the gladiators proved oblivious to every taunt, and as they strode towards the arena's entrance, their minds were locked into concentration on the combat to come; they attempted to uproot any treacherous trace of panic from their faces or bodies, since a gladiator who showed the least sign of dread or nervous hesitation would be cut down instantly by his opponent. Then, the underground cacophony of screams, bestial roars, whining sobs and maledictions abruptly fell silent as the gladiators emerged from the tunnels and entered the arena. The subterranean stench of terror fell away and the pristine early-morning air struck the gladiators' faces. After the dank darkness of the underground passages, the sudden daylight blinded them, and for a moment, there was no sound to be heard, either in the arena or in the vast expanse of Rome itself. Every eye in the crowd was fixed upon the gladiators, from the gaze of the basest scum to that of the emperor himself. Then, massive sonic shock-waves resonated in spirals around the arena, pulsing outwards and threatening to send that building, and the entire city around it, crashing to the ground. The gladiators heard the crowd's great chant: "Gladiator! Gladiator! Now kill! Now kill! Rome demands it!"

The ultimate paradox of the gladiator's life lay in the contrast between that momentary acclamation and the lower-than-zero status which he habitually held in Roman society. As each gladiator made his ritual greeting to the emperor – "Those about to die salute you!" – he possessed an exceptional nobility and purpose which still echoed with the original role of the gladiator as the liberator of the Mediterranean world from its malicious deities. But as soon as he stepped outside the arena, the gladiator was back in his usual sphere of unrelenting tedium, scorn and buggery. Innumerable mosaics and carvings were created, throughout the Empire, depicting gladiators in the heated combat which was their authentic element, with one elated gladiator about to plunge his sword or trident into the exposed throat of his exhausted opponent: such images served as exciting sex aids for their wealthy owners. But the everyday life of the gladiator generated no compulsive engagement for anybody, apart from the sexual hangers-on who dreamed of having their vaginas and anuses full of the fresh semen of the same gladiator that they were now seeing in the process of being cut into bloody pieces of slaughtered meat in the arena. Some gladiators had futile ambitions to finally leave their profession and become farmers or slave-drivers, but only the most unexceptional among them actually received the wooden sword of cowardice from the emperor which showed that they had been allowed to cast off their gladiatorial status. Few actually made anything of their subsequent lives, and it was a familiar sight in the most backward parts of the Empire to encounter a wandering ex-gladiator, destitute and starving, who was ready to commit any act of murderous or carnal depravity in exchange for a dry hunk of spelt-flour bread. Like *ronin*, the masterless-samurai class of seventeenth-century Japan, the former gladiators led broken lives of nostalgia and bitter regret, belatedly wishing that they could have died in the arena while hearing the rabid roar of the crowd as their ultimate sensory input. The best of the gladiators would never leave their profession, tenaciously fighting until the end, and finally exiting the cursed world in a blaze of glory.

The number of gladiators whose lives were expended in the most profligate of Caligula's spectacles could be enormous, extending into thousands of pairs of fighters. His miserly predecessor, Tiberius, had kept the crowd rationed to under a hundred gladiatorial pairings for each games, and prior to that, the first of the Julio-Claudian emperors, Augustus, had only managed a maximum of six hundred pairs. As in all domains, atrocity soared under Caligula's control of the gladiatorial combats. The main provider of the finances for each games, known as the "editor", was invariably a fabulously wealthy individual who wanted to ingratiate himself with the emperor by providing an event whose sheer excess, in terms of both violent deaths and luxurious attention to spectacular detail, would make even the most extravagant of previous games appear parsimonious by contrast. The emperor would lavishly reward any outstanding "editor" who managed to provide him with a new dimension of sensory overkill, often by simply re-assigning entire tracts of the Empire to be the lucrative fiefdom of that ambitious aristocrat or corrupt senator. The current ruler of the territory would usually find himself being inexplicably crucified or roasted alive, in order to ensure that he would neglect to dispute the new arrangement. Although the "editor" was nominally in charge of arranging the contents of the games, it was the emperor himself who had the final say; some emperors even took on the role of "editor" themselves if they wanted to stage a particularly spectacular carnage. The technical details of the spectacles were left to the most ingenious of the owners of gladiatorial schools to devise, and tens of thousands of engineers and designers from throughout the Empire were entrusted with making sure that the staging of the gladiators' entrances and exits – and their confrontations with suddenly-appearing wild beasts such as ravening lions and cougars – were synchronised in such a way as to drive the crowd into the most berserk frenzy imaginable. Innovations such as multiple-bladed decapitating machines, designed to harvest the heads of victims planted in the sand to neck level, were a further provocation to orgiastic abandon.

Once each of the combatants had approached and saluted the emperor – entrusting his life to the most arbitrary, divine caprice – and had received a lascivious wink or languid gesture in return, depending upon whether the muscled physique and easily-discernible penis of the gladiator appealed to the imperial eye, all of the gladiators then gathered together and began to form a procession which circuited the borders of the arena's combat zone. The gladiators were grouped into distinct factions, each armed with a different array of weapons; the combats almost always matched a gladiator with one set of weapons against another with a dissimilar set. One faction had their bodies covered almost entirely in protective leather and metal costumes, and carried small, circular shields, along with sabres and daggers; another faction appeared almost naked, with only miniscule loincloths pulled tightly over their sexual organs, and carried long, oblong shields and hefty swords. The gladiators removed their heavy helmets for a moment, allowing the straining crowd to pick out their favourites, as they screamed in wild adulation. Because each gladiator only appeared in the arena at intervals of every four to six months, the crowd eagerly convulsed with the fulfilment of lengthy anticipation whenever it recognized the face and body of an exceptional or preferred combatant. And the gladiators themselves were invariably eager to start fighting, after their long months of forced seclusion and mind-numbing monotony in the sex-reeking barracks. Although they often formed brusque, monosyllabic friendships with their fellow gladiators in those confined quarters, the raw elation of the arena instantly shattered any such bonds, and the eyes of the gladiators scanned their adversaries with excoriating menace.

Although the combat pairings of gladiators were ostensibly determined at the last minute, and left to chance, with a drawing of lots, this was entirely a bogus facade. The combats had actually been decided weeks beforehand, painstakingly arranged in order to provide the crowd with a grandiose spectacle of well-matched and gruelling combats, interspersed with instances of the most gratuitous killing. It was essential, over the long day in the arena, to maintain the crowd's level of acute cardiac adrenaline, and that could never have been left to chance. The crowd would swiftly turn against any "editor" who failed to provide them with a sufficiently intricate neural thrill coupled to the unrefined butchery which they craved; any badly-managed spectacle would usually result, at the end of the day, in the "editor" himself facing public disembowelment and simultaneous crucifixion in the centre of the arena, as a suitable compensation offered to the restive crowd by its emperor for lax or disappointing entertainment. The gladiators were informed of the running order and combat pairings several days in advance, at their barracks, in order to give them the opportunity to thoroughly bugger their opponent into subjugation as a prelude to the more murderous part of the confrontation. So, while the charade of the drawing of lots went on, the gladiators would look at one another with raised, blasé eyebrows, while the gullible crowd waited with baited breath.

After the combat pairings had been announced to the crowd, drawing from it gasped exclamations of pleasure or frustration, the gladiators would make one final processional circuit of the arena, before the combats started. A nervous gladiator making his first appearance would often involuntarily glance upwards, towards the high tiers of the arena, and see endless swathes of plebeian scum with their faces contorted in anticipation of the carnage to come; this was invariably a mistake, since the sight of that moronically salivating human debris would unfailingly terrify the young gladiator, coating his face with a sweat of abject fear, and ensuring that he would become the moribund combatant, unceremoniously carried out from the arena, feet-first and open-arteried, within the next few minutes. The more experienced and nonchalant gladiators knew never to look up at the crowd until their bout was over, by which time everything would be settled, and they would either be dead on the ground or else at the receiving end of a momentary torrent of exhilarating adulation. Finally, two of the gladiators would step forward. After a prolonged session of eye-to-eye glaring as they circled each other's fast-breathing bodies, their feet kicking up the earth and dust of the arena as though in utter derision of their opponent, the two gladiators finally closed in on one another and the combat began.

Not all combats were evenly matched. Often, to give the crowd a brutal sensory rush of the most invigorating kind, and to rapidly moisten its collective sexual organs in preparation for the more virtuoso performances to come, the day's bouts would commence with several examples of pure atrocity. A grizzled old gladiator with a hundred victories under his belt would calmly face a beardless, inexperienced gladiator who, only a short time before, had been herding pigs in the Calabrian hills, prior to receiving "the true call" to Rome. The young gladiator would make a show of curling his lip in derision at his relentlessly advancing opponent, and would execute a textbook defence with his shield, but the elderly gladiator would know just the right moment to feint to one side, exposing the young gladiator's throat to attack as he attempted to counter his opponent's ruse. In the very same second that the young gladiator realised that he had been tricked, he would find the blade of his adversary's sabre had been embedded six inches into his gullet. Few of those combats were offered for the arbitration of the emperor's thumb, since they had their place in the day's programme as foregone conclusions. The expression of the young gladiator's eyes would metamorphose in an instant from defiance to a look of total incredulity as the indented blade of his opponent's sword severed every major neck artery in a skilled sawing motion, sending vast gouts and spurts of arterial blood in carefully choreographed patterns around the arena. A skilled gladiator could divest his opponent of fifty per cent of his total blood content in the space of five seconds, but the mark of a truly top-rank gladiator was the ability to direct that pumping blood-flow into aesthetic configurations: the name of the emperor could be spelled out on the sand and dirt of the arena floor, and alongside it, the shape of the imperial Roman eagle itself would appear in black-red lines of blood. The young gladiator would then discover that, with the final adept movement of his artful opponent, he had been completely decapitated. The ultimate test of his adversary's skill would be to make the severed head fall to the ground in such a way that its position exactly dotted the single "i" of the revered name "Caligula", inscribed in blood. In the few seconds before the blissful unconsciousness of death set in, it only remained for the lips of the young gladiator's severed head to silently mouth the emperor's name, while the headless body itself slowly slumped to the ground in a blood-sodden tangle of limbs. The crowd would experience a moment of soaring neural ecstasy as they watched the young gladiator's summary execution, but that gratuitous sensation rapidly diminished, and they would begin to whistle and hoot for more punishing demonstrations of slaughter.

The combats then began in earnest. In many of the pairings, the weapons at one gladiator's disposal would necessarily put him on the defensive, so that he had to keep parrying his opponent's sword blows with his shield, until the moment came when the sheer intensity of those blows had exhausted the opponent. The defensive gladiator could then reverse his strategy and advance, charging down his fatigued opponent and gaining the upper hand. The crowd would follow every nuanced twist and turn of the combat, entranced, emitting collective exclamations, gasps of amazement, grunts of indignation and screams of approval as the bout progressed. In other, more evenly matched permutations of weaponry, the gladiators would struggle for long minutes on end in an intricate exchange of sword thrusts and counter-movements, until one proficient or unexpected blow would deeply penetrate flesh, with a sudden hissing sound that the crowd knew and loved. The wounded gladiator would then sit back on one heel with his eyes fixed on the ground; his adversary positioned his sword at an angle against the exposed throat. The vital moment had arrived for the imperial adjudication, and all eyes in the arena turned towards the emperor.

The emperor's thumb was the most crucial and most capricious organ in the entire arena. If the combat had come to an abrupt conclusion, the emperor would often be caught with his thumb, together with the rest of his fist, embedded in the anus of an exquisite young slave brought from Mesopotamia, between the Tigris and Euphrates rivers, where civilization had originated and muscular rectal elasticity was highly prized. The emperor would then have to retrieve his thumb at short notice, much to his dismay; such interruptions would usually provoke a psychotic fit of imperial petulance that led to a firmly down-turned thumb and the gladiator's immediate demise, whatever the degree of courage he had displayed in the combat. But, on most occasions, the emperor would meticulously gauge the mood of the crowd before making his decision. That mood could never be judged in advance, and because of the crowd's integral perversity, it could often take unexpected forms: the most inept or cowardly gladiator could receive collective roars calling for his reprieve, while a gladiator who had shown mettle of the highest order could dissolve into sobs of anguish as he heard the crowd braying in unison for his demise: "*Jugula! Jugula!*" It was invariably the lowest human dross on the upper tiers of the arena who determined the entire crowd's decision, and the deviance of the plebeian scum's verdict would often result from their having been too distant, poised high above the arena, to have seen exactly what had happened in a particular bout; occasionally, too, they were unsighted or distracted by wildly copulating figures who blocked their perspective on the action below. Ultimately, though, the mood of the crowd remained enigmatic and inexplicable, almost mystical in its contrary judgements and their vocal manifestation.

The emperor acquiesced on most occasions to the crowd's mass verdict, however bizarre or illogical it might appear to be; at such moments, an attempt by the emperor to overrule the ferocious will of the crowd might well result in an uncontainable riot that would have seen him floating face-down in the river Tiber, minus his majestical testicles, before nightfall. But on the occasions when the crowd hesitated, or vocalized a split decision, the emperor would seize the opportunity to exert his own perverse authority. He would allow his thumb to waver in a horizontal hold for minutes on end, each slightest tremor eliciting gasps from the crowd's one hundred thousand gaping mouths. Then, he would suddenly twist it upwards or downwards as though impelled by a definitive muscular spasm. It was divine will in operation. The gladiator who received a negative decision always took the imperial verdict in good heart, and, still sitting back on one heel, now nonchalantly tilted his chin up to the left, baring his pulsing artery to the victor, inviting him to slice through it. He would also tightly grip the victor's muscled thigh with both hands to steady himself with one final carnal gesture, and then nod his head. The victor would gruffly return the nod, and execute the blow in one movement, providing a dignified and relatively painless death. The expiring gladiator would tense his grip on his opponent's thigh in a momentary, orgasmic paroxysm, then release it and pivot backwards to sit down, his arms folded and his throat unleashing great spurts of blood, calmly waiting to die.

However, the emperor was sometimes faced with more intricate decisions and dilemmas at the termination of gladiatorial bouts. If the two gladiators were evenly matched, forty or even fifty minutes of gruelling but inconclusive combat could pass by, and the crowd would grow increasingly restless at the lack of a lethal resolution. Neither of the gladiators would want to subjugate himself before the other, since they knew that such an entrenched combat would ultimately have alienated the crowd, which required a steady regime of at least three eviscerations and two decapitations per hour. Finally, the emperor himself would have to step in to call a halt to the combat, by formally accusing both gladiators of the crime of "professional tedium"; they would then face one another and, at a signal from the emperor, simultaneously cut one another's throats and fall dead together. The insoluble dilemma posed by this outcome was that the victorious gladiator of a combat pair was invariably required to remain in the arena and immediately fight one further bout; when no victor survived, this was impossible. If it transpired that the locked gladiators were among his favourites, the exasperated emperor could simply gesture dismissively at the combatants, ordering them to suspend their bout until a later date, and then throw bags of low-denomination coins among the plebeian detritus in order to distract their attention from such a breach of protocol.

A less intractable dilemma for the emperor occurred when a gladiator, usually on one of his first outings in the arena, would lose his nerve completely and run away from his opponent, battering with his fists on the unscalably high barriers which divided the scowling and hissing crowd from the blood-reeking combat surface. Only one outcome was conceivable in such a situation. The crowd would curse and murmur to one another: "*Hoc habet*" – "He's had it". The emperor would nod brusquely, and the disgraced gladiator's opponent discreetly stepped away to one side. The crowd grew hushed, and then into the arena strode a golden-costumed dwarf of appalling hideousness. He belonged to a remote hill tribe on the eastern edge of Armenia that had developed an astral level of brutality to compensate for their stunted growth and freakish appearance, the result of millennia of inbreeding. The condemned gladiator would blanche at the array of weapons brandished with an ultimate sophistication by the approaching dwarf. The gladiator's abject screams would then resonate far beyond the arena, echoing through the city and even the surrounding countryside, and after ten minutes, he would find himself reduced to miniscule cubes of hot flesh scattered over the dirt of the arena. The crowd watched the lethal display in awed silence, and then applauded respectfully as the dwarf urinated on the flayed human cubes and serenely retired from view.

After each bout of combat, a bald-headed and nightmarish figure, the "carrion man", clothed in tight-fitting black leather and carrying a long-handled silver hammer and a burning poker, entered the arena. He ritually pressed the poker against the sexual organs of the defeated gladiator to determine whether he was alive or dead. If the gladiator screamed, he was alive. If he remained silent, he was dead, and the "carrion man" would strike his forehead with the silver hammer to take possession of his soul, which the grim figure was charged with transporting to hell. On the occasions when a gladiator had received a debilitating wound which had failed to kill him but prevented him from continuing the bout, he would be unceremoniously removed from the arena, on a stretcher pulled by a pony, down to a subterranean annex known as the "finishing-off room". There, despite the gladiator's protests that he now preferred to continue his fight or wanted to be returned home to the barracks, a hulking horse-butcher hired specially for the purpose would eventually appear, and soon put paid to the maimed combatant with a few well-aimed strokes of a cleaver.

It was essential that no loose ends were allowed to subsist from the day's work in the arena. The end of each day of the gladiatorial games had to be marked by a zero degree of carnage, in order for the following day's combat to begin with a pristine aura of renewed purity. Hundreds of slaves abruptly appeared in the arena and hosed the bloody sand clean with floods of perfumed spring water; other slaves rapidly sorted out the severed body parts and assigned them to a collection of jute sacks. At the same time, the victorious gladiators would gather to salute the emperor once more, and then exited from the arena with the thunderous cacophony of the crowd's adulation still pulsing in their heads; they retraced their steps through the labyrinthine tunnels echoing with the now-desperate cries of the criminal prisoners and the religious cultists, and returned to their dressing room, where they would grunt at their fellow survivors. The emperor himself would sometimes call by on his way back to the palace to congratulate them, usually arriving at the point when they had removed their battered costumes of leather and were standing naked within a trickling sheath of steaming blood. He would distribute a few gold pieces to their eager hands. After his departure, the gladiators – abruptly scum once again – would anonymously sidle out from a rear exit of the empty amphitheatre and slowly make their way back to their barracks.

Many other acts of slaughter also constellated the games. These took three main forms: duels between criminals, the massacre of dissidents and religious fanatics, and chariot combats. On some occasions, these spectacles of out-and-out butchery were segregated from the gladiatorial combats, which still possessed some faint residue of their original sacred purpose and needed to be cordoned off from the more profane acts of carnage. As a result, the gladiatorial bouts and other events were then staged on alternate days of the games. However, this arrangement remained eminently flexible, with the gladiatorial combats often being evenly interspersed with other entertainments. And if the day's gladiatorial bouts had failed to yield the required death toll and if the desired lake of arterial blood had not collected on the ground of the arena, then all of the gladiators would be summarily dismissed with one obscene gesture of the emperor's fist, and it would be time for the real slaughter to start.

For the crowd, the criminal duels could prove as exhilarating in their way as the most skilful gladiatorial bouts. The overriding factor which provided the fascination of those duels was that they could never ultimately be won. Every duel comprised a gruelling fight to the death, and the victor of one pairing immediately had to confront a new opponent. Even if he was totally exhausted from the previous duel, only a matter of a few seconds would elapse before the next combatant was catapulted into the arena from the subterranean cages of the amphitheatre. Nothing convulsed the crowd with greater ecstasy than a demonstration of the futility of human existence – it served to give their ephemeral moment of pleasure on the tiers of the arena a thrilling edge, which always manifested itself in desperate acts of multiple copulation. Sperm spurted in greater intensity during the criminal duels than during any other element of the games. Even the young spectators who disdained sexual interaction while watching the gladiatorial combats – believing them to form a spectatorial experience that demanded total concentration – would reach frenziedly for the nearest penis and jam it into their anuses, as soon as the brutality of the criminal duels had whipped them up to a dangerous level of neural oblivion. The only certain outcome of the criminal duels was that they would leave no survivors. Their participants fought only to live on for a further few minutes, at most a few hours, and that brief extension to their lives would take the form of punishing hand-to-hand fighting of the most ferocious, inhuman kind.

Many species of criminal found themselves condemned to fight in the arena, but the overwhelming majority of the participants belonged to the plebeian scum of the Empire. This factor, too, added to the elation which the massed ranks of human dross in the crowd experienced, since they simultaneously gloried in the deaths of the criminals and also empathized with them – only a slender thread separated the crowd from the criminals down below. The legal code of the Empire had been conceived with such arbitrariness that offenders who had committed exactly the same crime could find themselves either condemned to death in the arena or else released with a mild caution, depending on the whim of the judge who heard their case and the bribes or sexual favours they could offer him. Anything from urinating in a public place to sporting an objectionable amount of facial hair could land the offender in lethal trouble. In the rural provinces, incest and sex with minors loomed temptingly large in every peasant's mind; such crimes merited immediate condemnation in Tingitana, on the south-western fringes of the Empire, whereas in the moronic northern province of Belgica, no one would dream of considering such everyday acts as criminal or even reprehensible. Criminal fodder for the arena's atrocities arrived from every far corner of the Empire, but many of the citizens of Rome itself also fell victim to the impenetrable twists of the legal code as it was applied under the Julio-Claudian regimes. Occasionally, hapless senators and merchants became mixed in with the common scum in the criminal duels, especially if the emperor had seized their fortunes and wanted to subject them to a final humiliation before they exited from the cursed mortal world. The Empire's prisons remained almost empty for centuries, their contents dispatched for public disposal in the arena.

The criminal duels, like the gladiatorial combats, were organized by "editors", whose principal dilemma lay in ensuring that the duels would achieve the requisite level of eyeball-to-eyeball brutality. Nobody in the crowd wanted to see the two combatants simply throw their jagged swords to the ground and refuse to fight, or run screaming in terror to the edges of the arena to plead for mercy from the howling audience. One solution was to make the criminals ingest a powerful hallucinogen shortly before they entered the arena; this provoked a searing narcotic frenzy which gave each combatant the paranoid delusion that their opponent was the embodiment of Death itself, who had come to claim them. In all cases, the combination of fear and the feral rage induced by the hallucinogen propelled the two duelling criminals into an amateurish but engrossing fight. Other incentives were offered to the more reluctant criminals: if they refused to fight and turned their backs on their opponents in disgust, attendants immediately began to lash them with whips and to thrust white-hot branding irons towards their sexual organs, until they finally turned back to face their adversaries. But the crucial lure for the combatants remained the desire to stay alive, even just for a few more hellish minutes.

An endless stock of criminals was available in the arena's subterranea, and however rapidly the massacre progressed, more and more wild-eyed figures, invariably naked and armed only with a rusty but razor-sharp sword, could be projected out into the gaze of the crowd. Since almost all of the criminals were untrained in the use of weapons, they would attempt to inflict as many deep wounds upon their adversaries as possible, often simply making mad, lumbering lunges. Sometimes, one crazed criminal would knock the other to the ground, then gouge out his eyes or insanely throttle him. Unsuccessful contestants often ended up with their testicles between their teeth. The crowd loved the ludicrous criminal duels, since unlike the more predictable gladiatorial combats, there existed no set rules, no codes of conduct and no dignified deaths: it was utter annihilation executed in the most clumsy, bungling way imaginable – the equivalent in the Roman era to the no-budget exploitation film, preferred by its adherents to hackneyed and sanitized Hollywood product.

At the end of the duels, one combatant necessarily remained alive; in a few rare instances, a criminal who was particularly skilled in swordplay or driven by unstoppable ferocity could survive from end to end of the day's combat, notching up hundreds of kills. The crowd would usually spit out the most malevolent obscenities and derision at the criminals, but, if one criminal showed special resilience, the plebeian scum would gradually get behind him and begin to applaud him at each victory. In the face of imminent death, carried along by the vocal adulation of the crowd, the blood-spattered criminal would suddenly experience contrary sensations of hopelessness and euphoria. He would look upwards in dazed disbelief at the precipices of the arena's tiers, packed with endless swathes of slavering and copulating scum. High up, above the hundred thousand steaming human bodies, a patch of blue sky appeared to indicate the faint possibility of a reprieve. He would triumphantly throw his arms in the air, as though claiming the status of a victorious gladiator, and look with pleading eyes towards the emperor. But it was useless: he was already condemned. Once he had massacred his final criminal opponent, a silence would fall upon the arena. An eight-foot-tall gladiator would appear, wearing an enormous black metal helmet and full visor, and swinging a mighty two-handled axe around his head; he advanced rapidly upon the now-cowering criminal and cut him cleanly in two at waist or chest height, eliciting from the crowd a furious roar of ejaculatory exultation that ricocheted around the vast arena. The day's spectacle was over, and the satisfied crowd would be left with a final view of the arena strewn with several hundred ineptly butchered human carcasses. The survival rate of the criminal duels was absolute zero.

In the systematic decimation of the Empire's dissident elements and its religious fanatics, the preferred instrument of death was the wild beast. Occasionally, as a special treat for the crowd, an emperor would also pit gladiators against the beasts. The massive operation of capturing great numbers of ravening animals to be used in the arena's spectacles eventually rendered entire species extinct, especially in the then-lush forests, mountains and plains of North Africa, whose fragile eco-systems became transformed into arid deserts as a result. Big cats and bears of every kind constituted the particular focus of the search, but the sight of unusual and previously unseen beasts in the arena always sent the crowd into unprecedented fits of adulation for the emperor, who regularly dispatched expeditions of tens of thousands of hunters to bring back such novelties. The gathering of wild beasts for use in the arena became a major industry, with vast shipments of caged animals arriving daily from the far corners of the Empire. They were housed in a zoo adjacent to the amphitheatre, where they were kept in a semi-starved state to ensure that they would be avid to rip the bodies of condemned dissidents and mystics into shards of bony pulp in the shortest possible timespan. From every part of Rome, the animals could be heard roaring away at night, and those terrifying howls were easily audible in the subterranean dungeons where the magicians, revolutionaries and cultists spent their final nights on earth, chained together and subject to torture and humiliation, whenever their brutal jailers felt the compulsion take hold of them to commit acts of sexual atrocity.

The logic of employing wild beasts in the wholesale massacring of the Empire's wide range of enemies lay precisely in the terror which they engendered in their victims, and in the open-mouthed awe which their appearance in the arena inspired in the crowd's plebeian detritus. The animal used most frequently in the arena was the legendary Libyan lion: the most magnificent specimens of this mutant species grew to eleven feet in length, with enormous paws armed with razorsharp claws of sabre-size dimensions; even their engorged testicles were as large as a man's head. The Libyan lion was the ultimate killing machine, especially if deprived of its usual diet: in the wild, on the then-fertile terrain of the Idehan Marzuq, it could lay waste to two hundred wildebeests and ostriches at one sitting. Armies of slaves were expended in the capture of those majestic beasts – they were impervious to tranquillizer arrows, and the only way to subdue them was for a particularly handsome slave to present his shapely, exposed anus to the lion's mighty sexual apparatus; then, once the act of copulation (which invariably proved terminal for the unfortunate slave, due to unsustainable blood loss) reached its critical point and the lion was momentarily distracted, a gang of a hundred or more whooping slaves would wrestle the lion to the ground and throw a net over it. It was a delicate operation which often failed: the lion would escape again after making short work of decapitating the slaves with its monstrous maw. The captured lions could be pacified by feeding them with almost-infinite quantities of Armenian brandy, the addictive qualities of which put them into near-comatose trances of gurgling tranquillity and rendered them amenable to their long journey over the Mediterranean. But as soon as they reached the port of Ostia, at the mouth of the Tiber river, their intake of brandy would be abruptly ended, sending them into a state of ever-greater rampant fury which reached its pinnacle at the moment of their entrance into the arena.

It was essential for the well-being of the Empire that its enemies – everyone from dissidents and terrorists to zealous cultists and mystical fanatics of every kind – should make their exit in as undignified a way as possible, and the use of wild beasts provided the medium for that degradation. If the terrorists had been paired together in the same way as the criminal duels operated, the scope would have existed for all kinds of final statements of revolutionary vitriol to be yelled in the presence of the emperor and the gullible crowd. But, faced with an enraged and slavering Libyan lion approaching at maximum velocity, its saliva-spurting maw already open to sever its prey's neck, few dissidents retained the presence of mind to call for a mass uprising of the downtrodden plebeian scum against the oppressive yoke of the psychotic Julio-Claudian regime. Most simply turned tail in terror and fled, thereby winning a millisecond of additional life before the lion caught up with them. For the crowd, such displays of foregone slaughter only provided a modest amount of excitement, even when the dissidents were allowed to group together in gangs of ten and were given weapons with which to defend themselves. The starving lion still annihilated them instantly, ramming two or three protesting heads into its dripping buccal orifice at the same time. The purpose of the slaughter was purely to rid the Empire of its rebellious elements, and the crowd had to accept that and to wait patiently for the more satisfying entertainments of the day's programme to begin. The arena's cleaners, however, always preferred the bestial carnage above any other element of the games, since the lions left no human remains to clean up, preferring to gulp down every last scrap of cracked human bone and assiduously lick up the pools of blood.

The decimation by wild beasts of the captured members of the Teutonic hordes could present special difficulties, since those heavily-bearded and scarred primitives knew exactly how to defend themselves against most onslaughts. They were the denizens of the vast Teutoburg forest, on the far side of the river Rhine, where the greatest-ever defeat of the Roman army took place in AD 9: three entire Roman legions had been mercilessly wiped out in an ambush within the glowering semi-darkness of the dripping forest, and the many thousands of dead bodies of the butchered Roman soldiers had, without exception, been defiled by the necrophiliac Teutons. The unlucky survivors of the battle were sexually tortured for years on end, with the captured Roman standards used as sex aids, before the devilish Teutons finally tired of their prisoners and killed them by bloody emasculation. The Battle of the Teutoburg Forest remained the Empire's own pre-eminent humiliation, and the sight of Teutonic prisoners in the arena invariably whipped the crowd into a frenzied fury. The problem was that the sturdy Teutonic fiends, many of whom stood over seven feet in height, were hard to kill. And they were supremely indifferent to the deadly situation they faced in the arena, obliviously stomping around as though they owned the place, and directing obscene and provocative gestures at the crowd and even towards the emperor himself. Confronted with an assault by a crazed but lumbering bear, the unfazed Teuton would nonchalantly wait until the bear was breathing into his face, and then stun it with one mighty punch to the forehead, before strangling it to death. And as a lion or tiger leaped towards the Teutonic savage, he would suddenly thrust his fist into its open maw, grab its tongue, and twist it around sharply, thereby choking the beast to extinction. The only solution was to send into the arena those beasts which the Teutonic thugs had never seen before, and were unsure how to defend themselves against, such as Mediterranean bulls; charged by an enraged bull with its spiked horns aimed at their stomachs, the Teutons would soon find their intestines had been looped around their kneecaps.

In the massacre of the religious cultists, the potential existed for more compelling displays for the benefit of the atrocity-avid plebeian scum. The more resolute of the fanatics and magicians would stand their ground in the face of the approaching wild beast, loudly invoking their deity and insisting that the lion or other animal should be transformed into stone or dust. Few lions would be stalled by the cultists' imprecations, and would simply charge into the pompously proselytizing figures and tear them limb from limb. The only prisoners capable of halting a lion's onrush were the skilled magicians who knew how to execute a complex series of waving hand gestures and vocal expulsions that would instantaneously hypnotize the lion and render it docile. It would roll over onto its side, purring. The magician would then look around at the already moronically stupefied spectators and begin to direct the same effective hand gestures at the crowd itself. The spectacle's "editor" then had to act quickly, unleashing a further ten lions into the arena; they would encircle the magician, making it impossible for him to mesmerize all of them at once, and the magician would soon discover that his head had been summarily ripped from his body: his final sensory experience would be the reeking stench of a lion's gulping gullet, and his last sight would be that of its pulsing, scarlet oesophagus. Among the more notable leaders of sects whose members were slaughtered in the arena was Pachrates, who habitually rode around on the back of a crocodile and once spent twenty-three years in a darkened room learning how to transform a doorbolt into a robot; and Plotinus, who famously had himself burnt alive in a heavily-advertised performance for which the spectators had to buy expensive tickets, and then reappeared some days later in the form of a snake. Part of the crowd's fascination with the spectacle of the martyrdom of fanatics stemmed from the fact that the uninspiring Roman gods themselves formed an amorphous, barely tangible collection; as a result, the bizarre range of religious sects – and the delusional hold they exerted on their adherents – intrigued the crowd, and even interested those authoritarian figures in charge of designing the Empire's power regime. After all, the most supremely bizarre and factional of the cultists' obsessions eventually came to be adopted as the Empire's official religion, in a cold strategy of power preservation that saw the emperor change his job-title to that of "pope", thereby preserving the corruption and atrocity of the Empire intact into the Dark Ages.

The chariot combats required a great degree of skill and training, and those criminals or dissidents condemned to pursue a career as a charioteer could survive for several years in their profession, if they mastered the strategies by which they could adroitly slice their opponent into several pieces, or else see him jettisoned from his chariot to crumple into a mangled mass of pounded bones. Enormous sabres were attached at horizontal angles to the chariots' wheels; a proficient charioteer would attempt, on one circuit of the arena, to knock his opponent out of his chariot by jolting against it from behind, and then, on his next circuit, to cut his adversary cleanly in two at waist level, as the dazed victim tried to stagger to his feet. The chariots would also crack against one other in ferocious splinterings of wood and metal, as the charioteers attempted to shatter one another's wheel axles. If the wheels broke off, the chariot catapulted into space; the foaming horses veered off in another direction while the charioteer tried to stay inside the rapidly crumbling box of wood in which he stood. This was called a "shipwreck". If he fell out of his chariot, the combatant faced certain death from being crushed under horse hooves or being exposed to the whipping sabres of oncoming chariots. But if he remained in his stalled chariot, he would then be rapidly decapitated by a sword blow aimed by a passing charioteer. And the flimsy boxes in which the charioteers rode provided no protection in the event that the driver collided with the barrier which separated the track from the crowd, so that his body would be compacted at high speed against that wall, instantly disintegrating in a scarlet liquid pall of bloody pulp that spattered upwards and drenched the closest spectators. The spectators had to keep scanning the entire expanse of the arena's killing ground with their eyes, since a deluge of blood could appear anywhere, at any moment, as the twenty to thirty chariots thunderously made their invariable fourteen circuits of the track. The rare charioteer who managed to survive a crash at full tilt unscathed was soon pulled to his feet by his assistants, the "*agitatores*", and given a restorative drink made principally from the crushed dung of a wild boar, the recipe for which had been devised by the emperor himself. Then the charioteer, invigorated, was given a new chariot and immediately pushed back into the race.

A series of chariot combats often filled the very last day of one games, since they required extensive modifications to be made to the arena, with the demarcation of the race track around its edges. But chariot combats also took place outside the arena, in a special stadium constructed solely for that purpose; it could accommodate three hundred thousand spectators, far exceeding the already vast capacity of the arena. And since the stadium was made of wood, it could be enlarged whenever the emperor judged that the chariot combats should be made even more spectacular, under the eyes of yet more of the insatiable plebeian scum of Rome. Around the stadium, hundreds of prostitutional huts sprang up, each catering to a different sexual deviancy; but the spectators also lost no opportunity to stage sessions of mass copulation and buggery on the tiers of the stadium itself, whenever the breakneck velocity of the chariot combats' murderous impacts pushed those spectators beyond their maximum neural threshold, into a pulsing sensory terrain where only multiple acts of lustful copulation with strangers could calm their rabid fever. The chariot combats attracted a very young audience who dressed stylishly for the occasion, in anticipation of the sexual furore in the stadium which was certain to result; the women wore bright robes which allowed their neighbours glimpses of achingly-erect nipples and shaven, semen-leaking vulvas, while the men showed off their straining penises through intricate folds in their own robes.

But even so, the stadium for chariot combats lacked the compulsive aura of slaughter and fornication which the gladiatorial arena generated to white-heat intensity. The plebeian crowd was always contented to the utmost degree when the games took place within the echoing precipices of the arena: the undisputed domain of the gladiator.

CHAPTER THREE
COMMODUS:
IMPERIAL DELIRIUM

Over a century after the deification and slaughtering of Caligula, another god-emperor staged a reign which attempted to match the ferocious intensity of Caligula's grandiose and murderous era: Commodus. And Commodus's reign, above all, epitomized the obsession with the cult of the emperor as gladiator which had begun with Caligula. Like Caligula, Commodus ruled with psychotic abandon, allying himself with the crowd and treating the Senate with lethal contempt. And the most direct way to activate the pulsating neural elation of the crowd was for the emperor himself to take on the costume of the gladiator, and to receive the thunderous adulation of the plebeian masses as he circled the arena, throwing his arms in the air after a crushing victory over a mercilessly butchered opponent. Caligula had only ever appeared in the arena less than a hundred times, since his competing commitment to headlong debauchery demanded such a large part of his dutiful attention. But Commodus undertook many thousands of gladiatorial combats in the arena, and massacred beasts wholesale with a professional skill and commitment which the buggery-addled Caligula had never managed to achieve. Commodus succeeded in literally fusing together the arena with the palace, by majestically living in the arena itself and scrambling together the two brilliant destinies which convulsed the Roman Empire: those of the emperor and the gladiator.

Like Caligula, Commodus spent much of his childhood with the brutish Roman legions on the northern military front, along the Rhine and Danube rivers. In the century since Caligula's reign, much had changed in Rome itself – for one thing, the Julio-Claudian dynasty had expired in a crescendo of conspiracy, buggery and murderous excess, and the Antonine dynasty now held power – but on the northern frontiers of the Empire, the picture was dispiritingly similar. The rampaging Teutonic hordes still threatened to swarm across the Rhine and Danube to pillage and decimate Rome, and the emperors continued to formulate immense battle plans that would see the bestial Teutons defeated and ground into the dirt of their murky lands. Commodus's father, Marcus Aurelius, had been emperor since AD 161 and was noted for his sour demeanour and relentlessly grim view of human existence; he believed that he had missed his vocation, and that he should have been a philosopher rather than an emperor. In the swampland camps beside the Danube, surrounded by his boorish legionnaires and taunted by the obscenities that were incessantly hurled by the surly Teutons from the far side of the river, Marcus Aurelius found solace by ensconcing himself in his tent and philosophising. He was especially pleased with his own theory of sex, which took him many years to formulate: "Copulation is friction of the members and an ejaculatory discharge." But when he attempted to share his brilliant wisdom with the unrefined legionnaires, they simply rolled their eyes. His son, Commodus, also found it hard to indulge his austere father's vocational deficit and his dour view of an emperor's responsibilities and mission. Commodus, from his early years, had desired the lavish splendour of imperial glory and the exhilarating mass carnage of the arena. But Marcus Aurelius was intent on pursuing his duties on the dank northern frontier, hoping that he would eventually be able to divide the savage Teutonic tribes and conquer their godforsaken lands, thereby annulling forever their threat to the Empire.

In AD 180, Marcus Aurelius and his generals were planning a final push over the Danube, intending to scorch their way northwards with an apocalypse of fire across the gloomy forests and plains of Germany, until they reached the Baltic sea.

But Marcus Aurelius, then fifty-nine years of age, was exhausted from his long years of campaigning and fell fatally ill, having contracted the plague, which was rampant in northern Europe at the time. He called Commodus to his sickbed, and told him that he would soon assume imperial power. It was the first time in the entire history of the Empire that dynastic power was to pass directly from father to son; in every other instance, the sons of emperors had been brutally massacred or had died prematurely, usually poisoned by conspirators or even by their own parents. Although the dissolute and incipiently-psychotic Commodus was clearly poor material for the responsibility of imperial power, Marcus Aurelius could not miss the opportunity to prolong his dynasty. He instructed his son to follow the advice of the Senate, and to preserve the power system under which the wealthy Roman merchants and aristocrats subjugated the poverty-ridden plebeian scum. He also made his son promise that he would work unceasingly to enlarge the boundaries of the Empire in every direction. He then issued a proclamation, announcing that his heir was "the Rising Sun of the New World", and, his favourite works of philosophy by his bedside, he settled down to die. But the plague was an excruciatingly slow death, gradually rotting the internal organs and transforming the face into a pulsing mass of black boils that would suddenly emit great geysers of stinking orange pus, spattering everyone in the vicinity. Commodus finally grew so sick of looking at Marcus Aurelius's face and trying to dodge the ejaculations of pus, and so impatient to set out for Rome to receive the crowd's adulation, that – after sending everyone from his father's tent and putting on a pair of thick protective gloves – he throttled the emperor into oblivion. It was 17 March AD 180. Although it was evident that Marcus Aurelius, with his protruding tongue and bulging eyes, had been murdered, most of his generals decided to follow his wish that his son should succeed him, and they proclaimed Commodus emperor. Commodus's first imperial act was to announce his father's deification.

Commodus was nineteen years of age at the time of his accession; born in AD 161, he had been the survivor of male twins, his brother having died young. The birth of the imperial twins had been celebrated in Rome as promising the arrival of an unparalleled age of glory; when one twin died, that promise abruptly metamorphosed into a glowering malediction. Commodus was now eager to reach Rome as soon as possible. But, much to the new emperor's exasperation, he had to spend the first few months of his reign still holed up in the muddy, rain-drenched military camps, negotiating a truce with the grunting Teutonic chieftains. He had decided to abandon his father's grand scheme to invade the dank Teutonic homeland. One by one, the malodorous savages passed through his tent in their woolly costumes, to offer their obeisance to him. To his horror, each chieftain expected the emperor to bugger him, to seal their agreement, and Commodus was kept busy for five months as the thousands of sub-chieftains and deputy-chieftains from the various tribal factions kept on coming. And by the time Commodus finally dealt with the last of the slavering Teutons, in September AD 180, new conflicts had already broken out along the Danube frontier, and it seemed that the truce would have to be sealed all over again from scratch. In the end, Commodus, his precarious neural balance now reeling in every direction, decided that he had simply had enough, and he abruptly set off for Rome with most of the legions, leaving the frontier still simmering.

The plebeian scum greeted Commodus's arrival in Rome with delirious celebrations; on 22 October AD 180, the new emperor entered the city at the head of an immense procession intended to mark the triumphant conclusion of the war against the rampaging Teutonic hordes. The crowd had despised the aloof Marcus Aurelius, especially detesting the way in which he had protected the wealth and power of the merchants and aristocrats, at the plebeian mass's expense. Marcus Aurelius had also opposed the gladiatorial combats and bestial massacres in the arena which formed the very centre of existence for the urban scum; the great arena had even been closed down, and had partially fallen into dereliction. After he had witnessed the crowd's adulation, Commodus magnanimously promised that they would witness spectacles in the arena which would put even the Julio-Claudian extravaganzas of sensory excess into the shade. In his initial dealings with the Senate, Commodus took a sly approach; like his true mentor, Caligula, he began by flattering the senators and promising to rule wisely. But the senators had so often found themselves being duped, and then butchered, by a new emperor that they suspiciously viewed the affable Commodus with deep distaste. And, in appearance, Commodus indeed offered a revolting sight: he was a freak of nature, with an immense, tubular swelling of blood-congested blue flesh at his groin that made his robes protrude by over twelve inches. The avid plebeian scum speculated whether Commodus's bulging robe hid a permanently-erect, magnificent imperial phallus, but they were disappointed to learn that the emperor's freakish appendage was located just above his much more modest sexual organ.

Commodus – who by now was rumoured to be keeping both male and female harems, each some 300 in number, for his private debauches – ordered the imperial engineers to renovate and enlarge the capacity of the arena. He also commanded that one entire side of the arena be transformed into an extension of his palace; sumptuous suites of rooms were installed as a kind of terrace, with their balconies looking directly over the killing zone. This enabled Commodus to literally live in the arena for most of his time. In the first years of his reign, he hired the services of the greatest gladiatorial trainers of the era, together with the most skilled hunters and chariot racers. When the arena was empty at night and the plebeian scum had dispersed, Commodus practiced incessantly under the illumination of great braziers arranged around the arena's tiers. The gladiatorial trainers imparted all of the intricate skills of their profession to him. Commodus undertook seven years of intensive work, for eighteen hours each day, his training suspended only when the arena was occupied by the magnificent spectacles which he provided for the plebeian scum. Before dawn, he would drive his chariot at high speed through the empty streets of the city, learning to effortlessly negotiate the sharp turns that often saw less adroit charioteers crushed into bloody pulp in the arena. Entire species of rare beasts imported from North Africa were decimated in Commodus's practice sessions, as he learned how to spear animals from a safe distance. By the summer of AD 187, Commodus had developed a proficiency in the arena that made him the equal of most professional gladiators; only the protrusion from his groin would have disqualified him from pursuing a successful gladiatorial career if he had not been emperor. Whereas Caligula's short reign gave him little time to hone his skills in the arena, Commodus was able to carefully refine his expertise under specialist tuition, until, in October AD 187, at the age of twenty-six, he was finally ready to step publicly into the arena, under the gaze of the crowd, and to receive its ferocious adulation.

Commodus arranged a spectacular series of games to mark his own entry into the arena. The massed plebeian scum jammed its way towards the upper tiers of the arena at dawn, suffocating and trampling many thousands of unlucky would-be spectators as they surged through the gates. After a build-up lasting the entire day, and with the frenetic crowd propelled into a collective state of near-apoplectic neural overdrive, Commodus finally appeared in the arena. Under the gaze of two hundred thousand rapt eyes, he contemptuously cast off his imperial robe of purple and gold silk; beneath it, he wore the austere leather costume of the gladiator. He then forced all of the senators to kneel before him and reverentially intone the words: "You are the master, you are the victor, and you always will be." Then, the ten greatest gladiators of the day formed a line in front of Commodus, and he instructed the crowd to choose which of them he should face as his first opponent. Fearful that they would see their adored emperor being immediately decapitated, the plebeian scum shouted out the name of the weakest among the gladiators; but, once they realised that Commodus had followed Caligula's brilliant strategy of allowing his opponent to use only a wooden dagger against his own razorsharp sword, they instead roared out the name of the strongest. After circling the nonplussed gladiator for several minutes, Commodus butchered him, then wheeled on the spot, his arms in the air, as the adulatory roar of the ecstatic crowd ricocheted its way in blistering sonic bursts around the arena. As the crowd exited through the arena's gates, which had only just been cleared of the human debris caused by that morning's crush, great showers of golden coins were thrown to them, and once again, thousands of the abject plebeian scum found themselves being mashed to unrecognizable bloody tissue under the resulting stampede.

On the second day of the games, Commodus decided to demonstrate his prowess in hunting, and slaughtered over a hundred bears in two hours, accurately hurling huge spears at the bellowing beasts from behind a human shield of slaves. Whenever he grew tired, a female Nubian slave, naked and over seven feet in height, would rush over to him with a revitalizing drink of chilled honey wine, served in a cup designed in the shape of a mace. Sometimes, he would display his hunting skills from one of the majestic balconies at the side of the arena that formed part of his palace. From this terrace, Commodus would launch javelins towards carefully positioned beasts, invariably felling them at the first attempt. He began one session of carnage by slaughtering five hippopotami, two elephants, eighteen rhinoceroses, and one giraffe within the space of an hour. After a short break, he then undertook the ultimate test of his hunting skills, massacring one hundred leopards with one hundred javelins, never once missing his target. Then, as a sort of reward to please the enraptured crowd, a swarm of terrified ostriches was released into the arena, running wildly from one side to the other; Commodus shot hundreds of crescent-headed arrows from a jewel-encrusted bow, cleanly severing the ostriches' heads from their bodies; the crowd howled in delirium as they watched the decapitated ostriches continue to career around the arena, their necks now spouting pulsing plumes of blood. Within twenty minutes, Commodus had annihilated every last bird.

But it was the gladiatorial combats that proved to be Commodus's abiding obsession, and over the last four years of his reign, he notched up twelve thousand kills. Apart from allowing his opponent only to use a wooden dagger, Commodus rigorously followed all of the arcane regulations governing gladiatorial combats. He continued to give the crowd the right to choose his adversaries, and insisted on being paid enormous professional sums by the aristocrats who patronized the games. All over the Roman Empire, statues were erected to the imperial gladiator Commodus, noting his death toll and his ability to wield his sword with his left hand, which was viewed as a sign of special distinction. But Commodus could become jealous if he believed that his supremacy in the arena was being threatened by anyone else, and over the final years of his reign, hundreds of hunters, charioteers and gladiators all found themselves being summarily executed when they attracted the crowd's attention to the detriment of the adulation shown to Commodus. The emperor's career in the arena formed an extraordinary achievement. Like Caligula, he had managed to comprehensively debase and pervert the entire status of imperial power – the gladiator was regarded as inhabiting the very lowest layer of Roman society. But, ultimately, Caligula's achievements in the arena surpass those of Commodus, since the almost infinite replication of Commodus's appearances and killings in the arena, together with his obsessive citations of Caligula's own atrocities (Commodus was certainly the first post-modern Roman emperor), finally diluted and diffused the scandalous impact inflicted upon the Empire by the spectacular vision of the emperor as gladiator.

In his rare excursions outside the arena, Commodus cut a striking figure. He declared early in his reign that he would never appear in public unless he was covered in blood, and made sure that his robe of purple and gold silk stank with human and animal blood whenever he visited the Senate to terrorize its members. He also wore a crown of solid gold, inlaid with precious gems collected from all over the Empire and even beyond its frontiers. Without warning, Commodus would stride into the Senate's meeting hall late in the evening, fresh from his day's kills, holding the severed head of an ostrich or flamingo in one hand, and his blood-caked sword in the other; then, he would stand in silence in front of the massed senators and glare murderously at them, scanning each face in turn. Occasionally, he would switch his gaze from the intact human head of a senator to the severed bird's head, with the connection made explicit by his glowering eyes. The vast majority of the craven senators whimpered in fear, while a scattering of more hardy characters returned Commodus's stare. Then, the emperor would abruptly break into a malevolent grin, as though the whole performance had been intended to taunt its audience, rather than to gauge which of the senators would be next in line for butchery. As with the games hosted by Caligula, Commodus's spectacles of gladiatorial carnage for the benefit of the plebeian masses were principally funded by the summary murder of wealthy senators and merchants, on one concocted pretext or another, followed by the confiscation of their entire assets. Over the course of his reign, Commodus's already-dire relations with the Senate deteriorated relentlessly. He brandished about a long hit-list of condemned senators, like those drawn up by Caligula. A few of the exasperated senators formulated a plot to assassinate the emperor, and entrusted one of their youngest members, Quintianus, with the mission of stabbing Commodus on his next visit to the Senate. But the verbose Quintianus became so over-excited when he confronted the unsuspecting Commodus that he decided to make a speech before delivering the fatal blow. He waved his dagger in the air and began, "We, the noble Senate, have decided to be rid of the vile tyrant Commodus..." By the time that he had reached the end of his fatuous declamation, Commodus's bodyguards had overpowered him, and he was taken away to suffer the most excruciating death (by systematic torture and gradual emasculation) ever inflicted in the history of the Empire. After that, Commodus refused even to acknowledge the existence of the Senate, other than as a focus for his strategies of income-generating slaughter. He naturally became increasingly paranoid about plots against him, and condemned his wife Crispina and his sister Lucilla to exile and then death for a suspected conspiracy. Other than his excursions to the Senate, Commodus almost never left his home in the arena; when he did reluctantly have to return to his main palace, usually to preside at lavish feasts honouring visiting despots who were allied to Rome, he appeared irascible, and blurted out exclamations and insults with a saliva-spattering incoherence that rivalled Caligula's own style of speech. On those forays, Commodus had a totally vacant and distracted expression; he was an exile in his own palace, and the alien world outside the arena barely existed for him at all.

Soon, Commodus had concluded that his own majestic body constituted and encompassed the entire Roman Empire, and that the imperial domain needed to be re-named accordingly. He began with Rome and its inhabitants, deciding that he would now become the creator of the city by instituting a total return to zero (clearly an inspiration for Pol Pot's experiments with Cambodia in the 1970s). In AD 190, the city's very existence was cancelled out on all documents, and Commodus proclaimed that he was himself the new founder of Rome, with the city now bearing the name "Commodus Colony"; its full name actually became "The Fortunate, Immortal and Universal Colony of the Earth, Created by Commodus", but the city's inhabitants preferred the shorter name. They themselves became known, along with the rest of the Empire's population, as the "Commodians". The ships which brought the essential grain from North Africa to Rome were named "The Fleet of Commodus", and the army become "The Legions of Commodus". With an advanced sense of irony, the emperor re-named the Senate "The Lucky Senate of Commodus". Once he had started his great work of reinventing the Empire, the elated Commodus deliriously issued proclamations in every direction. All space and time now owed its existence to him: he re-named the months of the year after the magnificent titles which he had awarded to himself, and declared that he had instituted a glorious new age of infinite happiness for all of the plebeian scum of the Empire. It was called "The Golden Age of Commodus".

Between his commitments to gladiatorial combat in the arena and his frenzied re-naming of the entire contents of the Empire, Commodus had no time left at all for the practical business of running his imperial domain. He delegated its administration entirely to his cronies, whom he chose at random and allowed a free hand. His favourite administrator was a former slave named Cleander, who devised an intricate system of corrupt administration exclusively devoted to generating wealth for himself and Commodus; the Empire was squeezed dry, to its furthest corners, and its wealth channelled into Commodus's arena and Cleander's dissolute lifestyle. Cleander also became supreme commander of the Roman legions but, because of the rigorous military policies set in place by Marcus Aurelius, little trouble actually occurred in the Empire during most of Commodus's reign. In AD 184, the rampaging Scots had tried to overrun the now-conquered Britain, but they were soon repulsed by the brutish Roman legions stationed there, and Commodus seized the opportunity to claim for himself the noble title "Britannicus", which had previously been held by Caligula. The only other trouble came in the following year, from the direction of Gaul, which had become a lawless colony, relentlessly criss-crossed by murderous hordes of pillaging brigands. One of the brigands' leaders, a charismatic former soldier named Maternus who had deserted from his legion, decided that he would travel to Rome with a few of his trusted associates in order to assassinate Commodus, with the aim of wreaking mayhem. But, once he had arrived in the city and was choosing the best moment to slay the emperor, the courageous Maternus was abruptly betrayed by one of his associates; Commodus himself presided over the spectacle of Maternus being dragged into the arena to be eviscerated by a pack of ravening Libyan lions. Otherwise, the Empire ran smoothly, its sole purpose now being to generate income for Cleander and Commodus. However, in AD 190, Commodus abruptly had Cleander slaughtered on a caprice, and from that moment on, nobody at all was in control of the Empire, which careered wildly towards calamity at full speed. Unlike Caligula, who was prepared to gave his life for the divine glory of buggery and incest, Commodus now had little time available for sexual activity of any kind, and certainly never considered fathering an heir to prolong the Antonine dynasty. After dispatching his wife,

Crispina, to exile and death, he had a beautiful mistress named Marcia, but totally neglected her; apart from brief sessions of cursory buggery with burly wrestlers in the imperial baths, his attention remained exclusively fixed on the arena's killing zone.

In the final part of his reign, Commodus resolved that he would transform himself into a living god, as Caligula had done. He had the brilliant idea that, by becoming a god, he would not need to tear himself away from the arena to copulate with Marcia in order to produce an heir, since he himself would now live and reign forever. Ever since he had become emperor, he had identified himself with the god Hercules, often appearing in the arena in the costume associated with that deity: he dressed in a lion's skin and aggressively wielded an enormous club. But Commodus now decided to try something more sophisticated. He was well aware of one of the myriad of bizarre religious cults that were proliferating across the Empire from Judea, "Christianity"; the idea it promoted of having only one god (rather than a swarm of them) appealed to Commodus, since he believed that the potential for corruption, manipulation and devastation contained in such a system of monotheism perfectly suited his own future plans. He therefore declared himself to be the monotheistic fountainhead of the entire universe, responsible for creating the Empire, the world, and all of space and time. But, unlike the magnificent self-deification of Caligula, the metamorphosis of Commodus into a living god failed to enthuse the plebeian scum of Rome in the way he had hoped. They simply wanted to see their emperor in the act of butchering the maximum number of human beings and wild beasts in the shortest possible time, while they elatedly crammed the tiers of the arena and unleashed a devastating sonic wave of adulation at the never-ending torrents of blood.

On 1 January AD 192, Commodus was due to appear in his gladiatorial costume before the subjugated Senate to receive its highest honours. But, the night before, he abruptly fell victim to his mistress Marcia, who had grown angry at his neglect of her. Commodus was always too busy becoming a god and slaughtering untold human lives to give her the sexual satisfaction she needed. In a fit of rage, she fed Commodus a piece of meat that had been dipped in a powerful soporific solution. Then, while the emperor lay sprawled in a semi-coma in the steam room of the imperial baths, Marcia persuaded one of her lovers, a brawny wrestler named Narcissus, to strangle Commodus. Narcissus then crept up behind Commodus and brutally garrotted him; Marcia had the satisfaction of finally seeing the blood-congested penis of the agonized Commodus swell up to its maximum purple elongation, before unleashing a torrent of terminal semen into her mouth as the gurgling emperor expired in a burning neural flash of orgasm.

The relieved survivors of the Senate gathered on the following morning and gloatingly cursed the memory of the deceased emperor for all eternity, just as their predecessors had done after the spectacular demise of Caligula. They decided that the body of Commodus should be attached to a rope and dragged at high speed through the city streets behind his own chariot, then thrown into the river Tiber as an admonition to the distraught plebeian scum (although, in the end, nobody could summon up the effort to actually do this). They issued a proclamation: "Let the memory of Commodus the parricide, the gladiator be obliterated! Let the statues of the gladiator be destroyed, and his memory wiped out for all time!" However, it would be the Senate, rather than the assassinated emperor, who would be forgotten: Commodus remained an invaluable source of inspiration to dictators and tyrants throughout the following two millennia, providing a prescient – and forever contemporary – revelation of the power of excess.

Commodus had spectacularly succeeded in utterly debasing and perverting the Roman Empire, and in reducing the revered position of emperor to that of dirt. On 1 January AD 192, the conspirators in Commodus's murder offered imperial power to one Publius Helvius Pertinax. 87 days later, the 66-year-old would-be tyrant was butchered to bloody shreds of gristle by the collective sword-blows of 300 soldiers. While his severed head was still impaled on a stake, in full view of the plebeian scum, the role of emperor was being summarily auctioned-off to the highest bidder. The prizewinner, an elderly and debauched senator named Didius Julianus, had even less time to celebrate his acquisition of imperial dominion over the entire civilized world. Within 9 weeks, he too had been gratuitously slaughtered. The next emperor, Septimus Severus, reigned from AD 193 to 211, eventually dying of illness – but not before there had been several attempts to murder him by his own son, Caracalla, who became another of the top-ranking monstrous tyrants in the history of the Empire.

Caracalla and his brother, Geta, became joint-emperors; within 11 months, Caracalla had brutally assassinated his hapless sibling. The first of the two principal atrocities which marked Caracalla's reign was the mass execution, without trial or cause, of all of his brother's supporters. In the early months of AD 212, some 20,000 citizens were killed in this way, callously slaughtered in the streets, the baths and in their homes. In May AD 215, Caracalla travelled to Alexandria, in Egypt, as part of a grand tour of the Empire. His second great act of atrocity took place there. The delusional emperor suddenly ordered his soldiers to slaughter all of the young men of the city, whom he believed had been mocking him; thousands of unarmed victims were rounded up and then summarily put to the sword in a great frenzy of emasculation, mutilation and rabid torture.

Caracalla finally met his untimely end in AD 217, on the road between Edessa and Carrhae, at the receiving end of a murderous gang of conspirators led by one Marcus Opellius Macrinus. Suffering from food poisoning, Caracalla abruptly halted the march to relieve his bowels at the roadside. As he crouched in the sand, straining, an assassin stepped up (the sound of his feet luckily muffled by a deafening blast of imperial flatulence) and plunged his sword deep into the tyrant's back. Caracalla's heart-blood spurted out in terminal arterial gouts, at exactly the same moment that a malevolent fountain of diarrhoea jetted from his raw, distended anus. It was a fitting image to mark the beginning of the Empire's final acceleration into rapid-fire atrocity and calamitous collapse.

CHAPTER FOUR
HELIOGABALUS:
BLACK SUN RISING

"Myth and utopia: the origins have belonged, the future will belongto the subjects in whom there is something feminine"
—Roland Barthes

"We are all celebrating some funeral"
—Charles Baudelaire, *Salon de 1846*

AD 218 – one year after the assassination of the emperor Caracalla by conspirators led by the usurper Macrinus. Encouraged by his Syrian mother Symiamira, the fourteen-year-old Heliogabalus had taken to making up like a girl, as well as to wearing the translucent gowns his mother would adopt for the entertainment of her lovers. For years, the androgynous youth whose real name was Varius Avitus Bassianus identified himself with the sun-god Elagabalus, worshipped at Emesa in the form of a black conical stone, universally believed to have dropped there from the sky. As blood of the Emesan dynasty, Heliogabalus could count amongst his ancestors the hieratic Kings of Sohemias, as well as Samsigeramus and his son Iamblichus, the friend of Cicero. He could attribute something of his mystical sensibility to the temple of Emesa, and to the prophecies associated with the oracle of Belos at Apamaea.

Nothing would persuade the youth that he wasn't the living incarnation of the solar god. He knew this always in the way that a profound inner assumption strengthens in time to an absolute conviction. Heliogabalus's relations with the god at his

interior were mutually dependent, like the peach is to the stone
out of which it ripens. He had decided already that he would act
out the god's instructions, no matter how significantly these
dictates appeared to rupture the social fabric. Living with a god
threw Heliogabalus into violent mood swings. He could be
delirious with excitement or broken through a sense of dejection
that he wasn't equal to his calling. His manic tilt lifted him on
a long trajectory towards the sun.

He had known since childhood that his triumphant
moment would arrive. The incestuous sex he practised with his
mother was part of his initiation into divine appointment. When
he performed sacrificial rituals before the black phallic stone, he
realised he was feeding the unappeasable need within himself to
be recognised. And far more than recognised, worshipped.
Heliogabalus knew his power, and that if he concentrated his
psychic energies he would manifest the nuclear god at his core.
Being extraordinary was his innate prerogative, and revealing it
his secular mission.

Heliogabalus had to fight for his title as emperor. Born
the grandson of Julia Maesa, younger sister of the empress Julia
Domna, and the son of Sextus Varius Marcellus, who occupied
the rank of senator under Caracalla, his mother Symiamira
claimed that Heliogabalus's real father was the murdered
emperor. On the notion of that claim alone Heliogabalus won the
loyal support of an army anxious to depose the despotically
savage Macrinus from the imperial title.

War between the two parties broke out immediately after
a total eclipse of the sun, an event interpreted as a potent sign
by Elagabalus's priesthood. It is clear that the revolt was a
complete surprise to Macrinus, who misassessing the gravity of
the situation left his prefect Julianus to take the initial step.

It's hard to imagine the predominantly feminine
Heliogabalus inspiring confidence in the military, and we can
only surmise that his grandmother must have instructed him how
to acquit himself in the field. While Julianus was successful on
the first day, he squandered the advantage by the decision to
wait until morning before renewing the attack. Meanwhile the

opposition were busy pointing up the resemblance between Caracalla and Heliogabalus, and Maesa was quick to offer both sides money, if they were loyal to her cause. The result was that Julianus's troops promptly massacred their officers and went over to the enemy. Julianus was later hunted out, decapitated, and his head sent to Macrinus.

When news of Julianus's defeat reached Macrinus, and wishing to strengthen his reputation among the soldiers of the second Parthian legion who were stationed at Apamaea, he made his son Diadumenus, already Caesar heir-apparent, associate emperor. As an additional measure aimed at popularity, he restored privileges to the troops granted them by Caracalla; but no sooner had he effected these measures, than the malefic talisman of Julianus's severed head was delivered to the camp. Out of cowardice Macrinus fled back to Antioch, leaving the troops at Apamaea to go over to Heliogabalus. With Macrinus walled up in Antioch, Heliogabalus's troops took advantage of the open field to arrive within 20 miles of the city before Macrinus could engage them. If Macrinus's strength lay in his seasoned praetorians, then Heliogabalus's presence seems to have inspired in his inferior troops a courage and loyalty that were instrumental to defeating the opposition, most of whom either deserted or, won over by promises of indemnity or preferment, defected to Heliogabalus's side.

But before Heliogabalus could be proclaimed emperor it was necessary to track down Macrinus, who had fled from the war-zone. No matter that the army appears by this time to have been convinced of Heliogabalus's legitimate claims to the throne, there's something almost surreal in the idea of the troops proposing an ambiguously sexed Syrian youth, dressed in make-up, as their future emperor.

Realising that his life was on a short fuse, Macrinus burnt up a rapid trail of 750 miles via Aegae in Cilicia, through Cappadocia, Galatia and Bithynia, making Eribolus his destination, since Nicomedia was closed to him by the presence of Caecilius Aristo, a partisan of Heliogabalus. He was finally captured on or around June 17, by Heliogabalus's agents, who returned with their captive to Antioch. By the time the victorious party reached Cappadocia, they received news of the arrest and execution of Diadumenus, who had been sent by his father to the Parthian King for protection. After failing to commit suicide by jumping from a moving chariot, Macrinus was peremptorily and bloodily executed by a centurion at Archelais, 75 miles from the Cappadocian frontier.

On receipt of this news Heliogabalus sent an official announcement to the Senate, a message that travelling at the rate of 130 miles a day would have taken at least eighteen days to arrive in Rome. In the meantime, as a preventative measure to stop his troops looting and raping in Antioch, the soldiers were each given 500 drachmae as a token aimed at winning their continued loyalty.

But affairs were still unsettled, and as a consequence of his youth and inexperience, the management of Heliogabalus's immediate affairs, conducted at the temporary court in Antioch, fell to Maesa and her advisers. It was thought prudent for Heliogabalus to send letters to the Senate justifying his execution of Macrinus and his son, together with copies of the letters written by his predecessor to Maximus the city prefect, in which Macrinus's duplicity was unfavourably displayed. Copies of these letters were also sent to the army, along with an account of the risks encountered by the troops under Heliogabalus in the war they had just fought to proclaim him emperor.

Heliogabalus's position remained precarious, for while he had the support of the army in Egypt, the soldiers in Alexandria retained a sense of loyalty to the dead Macrinus. There was also uneasiness among the legions, and this resulted in a number of opportunistic attempts on the part of several officers to claim the throne. Amongst those who were brutally executed for being revolutionaries were Verus, a centurion's son successively championed by the third Gallic region, and Gellius Maximus, chosen by the fourth Scythian legion.

Acclaimed emperor by the troops on the morning of 16 May 218, Heliogabalus had taken the title Marcus Aurelius Antoninus as a means of asserting his hereditary claim to being the last of the Antonines. The title, however, was a distortion of his true identity as Elagabalus. He was a god first and an emperor second, and if temporal power as imperator was an asset, then it was largely so in terms of allowing the pre-eminently religious youth to argue for a monotheistic cult in a largely polytheistic empire. Even those close to Heliogabalus would fail to see that he was not so much providing a god, as incarnating that god in himself. It was this failure on the part of his subjects to discern the distinction that would lead within four years of his accession to his being chopped up by assassins and thrown into a rain-swollen Tiber.

Emperor at fourteen, and unsure really whether he was Caracalla's son or not. His mother had slept with so many men that his actual paternity was probably untraceable. Even his name Varius, implied promiscuity: both his mother's and his own. If he was the son of "various" men, then he himself would repeat the pattern established by his mother, and become a prostitute. Dressed in a long blonde wig, he who was a god would experiment with debasing himself dockside brothels in order to know what it was like for a man to be penetrated as a woman. He wanted to empathise so deeply with his mother's highly-sexed abandon, that he as a man would attempt to experience a pleasure similar to hers when she was possessed by a male lover. It was an act of supreme narcissism.

Secure in his title as emperor, Heliogabalus expressed no urgency about setting off for Rome. Rather he spent some months, first at Antioch, then later as the winter came on, at Nicomedia. After he had spent the winter in Nicomedia, living in a depraved manner and indulging in prolonged bouts of buggery and fellatio with male prostitutes, the army began to realise the error it had made in appointing Heliogabalus as emperor. While at Nicomedia, Heliogabalus also had his mother's lover Gannys executed, for he feared the latter was growing too powerful and would in time impose a threat to his title. It is unclear whether this act on Heliogabalus's part was one of jealous revenge, or a demand for a sacrificial victim to appease his god. Gannys' death is the first recorded murder instigated by Heliogabalus, and as such is a complex one in terms of psychological modalities. Gannys had been instrumental to helping Heliogabalus defeat Macrinus, but he had protested against the young emperor's quickly manifested depravities. Gannys was indubitably heterosexual. His attraction to Heliogabalus's mother was conditioned by lust and the scheming aspirations to realise power. Heliogabalus confronted Gannys with aspects of sexuality he would never experience: homosexuality and incest. Each time Gannys made love to Symiamira he would denarrate his libido, for his endeavours were naturally disproportionate to those of a son who impersonated a god. His dejection led to the fear of impotence or humiliation. He was powerless to make Symiamira resonate with his sexuality. Something interposed between their bodies. It was Heliogabalus's skin. When Gannys smelt it, he knew he would die. From this point on he had no appeal. He was emasculated. His hormonal drive was erased by an ambi-homo-polysexual-incestuous child-god. Death is easy after that. For Gannys it was a matter of pride.

Apart from Heliogabalus's homosexual promiscuity, there were other reasons why the imperial party's progress to Rome was so slow. The route was a bad one, and the procession demanded the sort of luxurious travel facilities and leisurely stops that were not in the interests of speed. Also coins, inscribed "Salus Antonini Aug." and "Salus Augusti", suggest that Heliogabalus fell ill some time between June 8 AD 218 and June 1 AD 219, and sickness may have in part been responsible for lengthening his stay in the East. Of the nature of his illness, we know nothing. It may have been sexually transmitted, it may have been of nervous origin, or it may have belonged to one of the viruses which were prevalent in armies at the time. In the interim Heliogabalus sent a portrait of himself dressed as a Syrian priest to Rome, to be put above the statue of Victory in the Senate house in anticipation of his arrival. This act of indiscretion in portraying himself in advance as a transvestite, suggests either disingenuousness on Heliogabalus's part or the desire to shock. Either way the decision was a wrong one.

Heliogabalus remarked to a friend: "What can be better for me than to be heir to myself?" And in terms of refusing to compromise, he meant it. The imperial cortège transported with it the black conical stone, brought from the temple at Emesa, to which Heliogabalus attached reverential status. The lithic symbol was rounded at the base and came to a point on the top, and was worshipped as though it had fallen from heaven; on it there were some small projecting pieces and markings, in which the people divined an image of the sun, since this was their desire. For the procession to Rome Heliogabalus had the stone set in precious jewels: diamonds, emeralds, rubies, sapphires. The fetish was placed on a chariot, and Heliogabalus at the reins orchestrated the muscle of six white horses in the slow, rainy haul to Rome. Already ascribing to himself the title *Invictus Sacerdos Dei Soli*, Heliogabalus dressed to defy any notion of gender. He was a transvestite who would like to give inner authority to his mutant appearance by becoming a transsexual. He wore a dazzling Persian tiara, and indecently for the times was dressed in gold silks. He had pencilled eyebrows, wore kohl to enhance his eyes, and white foundation toned with blusher. He sparkled with bracelets, necklaces and rings, and sported jewelled buckles on his fine leather shoes. No Roman emperor had ever presented himself in this way, not even Caligula, but to the outwardly effeminate Heliogabalus, his appearance complemented his understanding of himself as extraordinary. He was separate by way of a psycho-biology that acknowledged itself a god.[1]

Heliogabalus's assembled image of himself would make him too recognisably visible to his contemporaries. He would be overseen for his image, and underseen for its intrinsic value. The illusionist in him would be hated for choreographing special effects, a theme designed to partially conceal the nature of his mystic identity. Emperors are always in the spotlight. The prerogative of being Caesar carries with it the continual counterthrust of potential assassination. When Heliogabalus was massaged and fellated by a flavour-of-the-week rent boy he was inwardly aware of all the points at which he could be cut by a blade. The alert he felt at this apprehension, right down to intuiting the precise diagram of incisions to be worked into his body by organised assassins, kept him alive to the knowledge of a possibly violent death. He imagined his arteries were known to his enemies like the fingerstops on a flute to a musician.

Heliogabalus and his party probably reached Rome between July 11 and September 29, AD 219. The young emperor distributed money among the people to mark his arrival, an act repeated at the time of his marriage to Julia Paula that same year. He also prudently announced an amnesty for the many slanderous things said about both Caracalla and himself by people of all classes.

On his arrival at Rome, Heliogabalus immediately set about blueprinting plans for an eastern-style temple of the sun to be built to the Syrian deity Elagabalus. He thus neglected affairs of state in order to devote himself to a policy of religious syncretism. Of his monotheistic tendencies, it seems that he desired to transfer "the emblem of the Great Mother, the fire of Vesta, the Palladium, the shields of the Salii, and all that the Romans held sacred" to his particular temple on the Palatine Hill, near the imperial palace. This temple known as the Elagaballium was a huge colonnaded structure within a rectangular enclosure. To Heliogabalus, going there to worship was like steeping inside himself. The rites that Heliogabalus practised in his temple included "the barbaric chants which together with his mother and grandmother, he chanted to Elagabalus, or the secret sacrifices that he offered to him, slaying boys and using charms, in fact actually shutting up alive in the god's temple a lion, a monkey and a snake, and throwing in among them human genitals, and practising other unholy rites, while he invariably wore innumerable amulets".[2]

Our introduction to Heliogabalus's pathology is in the context of ritual. What is there in this youth's behaviour that justifies the transition from boy-god to monster? Are we to believe that the sex-addicted emperor also delighted in killing? Perhaps the mismanagement of gender in Heliogabalus, who wished above all to be a woman, found its compensation in the youth turning psychopathic.

Human sacrifice was more likely to be a simple part of his native religion. Heliogabalus also sacrificed large numbers of cattle and sheep on his altars. Part of Heliogabalus's plan was to undermine the importance of the military by having its leaders engage instead in religious practices. "The entrails of the sacrificial victim and spices were carried in golden bowls, not on the heads of household servants or lower-class people, but by military prefects and important officials wearing tunics in the Phoenician style down to their feet, with long sleeves, and a single purple stripe in the middle. They also wore linen shoes of the kind used by local oracle priests in Phoenicia."

Heliogabalus's devotion to his solar-based god was a visionary one. As the god's living incarnation he represented fire as the active energy promoting vision. Heliogabalus's mind was like a poet's in that he looked always to celebrate the marvellous in the ordinary, and to transform reality through the shape-shifting powers of imagination into a sensationally heightened dynamic. Heliogabalus's short duration as emperor corresponded in years to the formative state in youth, 14 to 18, in which the schoolboy Arthur Rimbaud – hundreds of years later – wrote the scorchingly hallucinated poems which continue to live as a visionary testament. Heliogabalus's theophanic embodiment of the god Elagabalus demanded a visionary's channelling of energies, in the same way as the child-magus Rimbaud appropriated the shamanic ideal as the tool of poetic identity.

Heliogabalus's contemporary Rome, while it was made stable by his lack of reform, nevertheless reflected the empire's general decay. The great plague of AD 167 had made permanent inroads on productivity, and this combined with Commodus's extravagance, the ambitious enterprises of Severus, and Caracalla's desperate liberality to the army had severely depleted the revenues. Macrinus had exacerbated the issue by way of his unsuccessful war with the Parthians. Unable to defeat the enemy, he had burdened the state with the double expense of maintaining an offensive as well as buying peace from the enemy. In the attempt to gain popularity Macrinus had proceeded to abolish the taxes which Caracalla had imposed on inheritances and manumissions, and so had further deprived the state of a healthy economy.

Under Heliogabalus, the government increased its volume of credit by depreciating the standard of the currency. Gold at the time was largely pure, and the aureus, which Caracalla had reduced to 6.55gr in 215, was successfully kept at this weight by Heliogabalus, who was quickly to become so extravagant in his personal tastes as to liquidate the entire economy.

Heliogabalus was obsessed by size. He loved men who were endowed with abnormally large cocks, and would send out procurers to the public baths with the task of finding him lovers who were suitably equipped with the most impressive genitalia. They would then be brought back to the imperial palace for Heliogabalus' sexual gratification. Fond of stalking the palace nude, save for the various perfumes and powders anointing his lithe torso, he also had the whole of his body depilated, with the sole object in life of appearing an object of desire to as many as possible. As Heliogabalus regarded himself as a woman, his preference seems to have been for rough trade with a difference. The young emperor's transvestite and homosexual propensities were displayed in exorbitant sex plays. Revelling in being buggered by the most enormous cocks in Rome, he "used to have the story of Paris played in his house, and he himself would take the role of Venus, and suddenly discard his clothes and fall naked on his knees, one hand on his breast, the other before his genitals, his buttocks projecting meanwhile and thrust back in front of his partner".

Heliogabalus's highly developed sense of camp, together with the histrionics at play in his dramatisation of himself as a woman, were all part of casting himself in a passive sexual role. Only by switching from the role of projectile male to passively receiving female could Heliogabalus feel complete.

Heliogabalus was understandably attracted to good looks. Not only did he have the public bathhouses searched for virile *onobeli*, but he went in nocturnal disguise with his pick-up party to search through the city's alleys and wharves for attractive youths (a practise previously employed by the emperor Nero). As a means of subverting the Senate, he would appoint rent boys, actors, circus performers and personal favourites to positions of power in the palace. He also took money for appointments, a corrupt practice that had him sell high-ranking positions like captain and tribune, legate and general, as well as procuratorships and significant posts within the palace. Ruled in part by a bias of same-sex attraction, Heliogabalus undermined state affairs by appointing a low-life fraternity to privileged ranks of office. But unknown to Heliogabalus in the euphoric adrenalin high of superimposing his sexual preferences onto government, he was already in the process of being watched. It was inevitable that the army should have begun to monitor the emperor's questionable behaviour. The army was the drive-unit behind keeping an empire in check. To jeopardise its power was to be more than observed with suspicion, it was to be scrutinised. From this point Heliogabalus would be unconsciously policed by an inquisitive lens. And the watching continued until such time as the emperor's accumulative outrages provoked the reprisal of his assassination. In that moment, the observed and the spectator would unite in a ritualised marriage of death.

Heliogabalus was, apart from Nero, the only Roman emperor to undergo a gay marriage. His partner was a Carian slave called Hierocles, who had once been the favourite of Cordius, from whom he had learned to drive a chariot. It seems Heliogabalus had met Hierocles while working as a prostitute in a notorious riverside brothel. Their initial encounter describes the psychological reversal of roles that seems to have been central to Heliogabalus's idea of sexual stimulus. The emperor disguised as a blonde prostitute sells his body for kicks to a charioteer, who in turn becomes his unlawful husband. And within the emotional arena of the marriage Heliogabalus insisted not only on being treated as a woman, but also on being beaten by his husband for his infidelities with other men. The masochistic emperor "wished to have the reputation of committing adultery, so that in this respect, too, he might imitate loose women; and he would often allow himself to be caught in the very act, in consequence of which he used to be verbally abused by his 'husband' and beaten, so that he had black eyes".

. Heliogabalus's private life consumed most of his energies. By substituting emotional theatre for reality, and by encouraging his entourage to likewise enter into same-sex marriages, he threatened by his example as emperor to dislodge the pivot on which the empire depended. Heliogabalus even established a court of transvestites, over which he presided as a queen. "There were in his entourage men who were depraved, some of them old and in appearance like philosophers, who used to wear hair-nets, and boast of their sex lives with their husbands."

It was inevitable given Heliogabalus's total identification with his anima, that his wish to be authentically feminine should have him argue the case for a transsexual operation. Accordingly, he asked the physicians to fashion a woman's vagina in his pelvic core by means of a surgical incision, promising them large rewards if they were successful. The sex-change that the emperor requested was refused by his doctors on the grounds of possible life-threatening mutilation. But the request had been made, and news of it soon filtered through to Heliogabalus's chief antagonist: the army. Fascinated by the idea of making some form of transformation to his genitals, Heliogabalus circumcised himself as a part of the priestly requirements of Elagabalus, and was said to have personally performed a similar operation on other initiates.

The emperor's own sexual identification seems to have been with the hermaphroditic. He would clearly have liked to have been both sexes, and to have experienced the penetrative powers of a man, as well as knowing the receptive facilities of a woman. In this way he would have realised sexual completion through the marriage within himself of male and female. Heliogabalus's psychological awareness of himself as the divinized representative of a god was part of the unconscious fantasia by which he lived. He saw his actions as adapted for the ultimate theatre, while the Senate interpreted his behaviour as that of a deviant and impostor. The colourful rituals with which Heliogabalus surrounded himself were viewed by the authorities as the irresponsible actions of someone unfit to rule. It wasn't only that Heliogabalus threatened to subvert accepted standards of gender, it was also that he challenged ideological rationale with the altogether more powerful dynamic of imagination. Governments, including his own, view imagination as a pathogen infiltrating a functional organism. Regarded as a feminine preoccupation, governed by the brain's right-side hemisphere, and so deeply subjective in its subliminal activities, imagination is viewed with suspicion by the majority of rationalists. Heliogabalus as a proponent of right-side brain activity, lived within the awareness of subjective reality. As an additional threat to a male-dominated, left-side, objectively reasoned Senate, Heliogabalus not only introduced his mother into the senatorial ranks, but set up a *senaculum*, or woman's senate, on the Quirinal Hill. This direct challenge to a male-dominated ethos, coming as it did from a pro-feminine emperor was a courageous attempt on Heliogabalus's part to revise the government, and to replace protocol with feminine characteristics like imagination and intuition, the revolutionary precepts of a black sun rising. And so Rome with its partially shut-down right-side brain hemisphere fought militaristically to maintain left-side control. Heliogabalus with his largely feminine preoccupations carried with him a threat to Rome far greater than an invading army, and that was the untameable power of imagination. You can't kill imagination, but you can kill the person carrying it, and Heliogabalus was to be watched with even greater scrutiny by imagination's opponents.

In the attempt to disguise his homosexuality, or as a compromise designed to satisfy his subjects, Heliogabalus married at least three wives, these being Julia Paula, Julia Aquilia Severa and Annia Faustina. What role, if any, these official wives played in his exhaustive sexual repertoire is open to speculation, biographical knowledge of them being at best inadequate and at worst non-existent. That there was probably little love shared by either partner in any of the three heterosexual marriages attributed to Heliogabalus, seems highly plausible, given the strength of his unofficial marital bond with the charioteer Hierocles.

It was in the year after his accession that Heliogabalus married Julia Cornelia Paula, whose father was the renowned juris-consul and lawyer Julius Paulus. The latter had climbed by successive stages from Praetor, to Prefect of Rome, to Prefecture of the Praetorium, and from there to senator. It's possible that the marriage was no more than a political move on Heliogabalus's part, for Julia was well over thirty at the time of the marriage, and certainly not commended for her beauty. As a transvestite, we would have expected Heliogabalus to have been attracted to women who were in some way his physical counterpart, rather than older women who were inferior to him in looks.

It is assumed that Julia had been previously married, and that she was already the mother of children at the time of her marriage to Heliogabalus. If the emperor's intentions were to use Julia as the vehicle to provide an heir to his dynasty, then the marriage was quickly annulled as childless. Whether it was Heliogabalus's inability to perform sexually or sterility on the part of Julia, the pretext for divorce issued publicly was that Julia carried a secret blemish on her body that proved offensive to the emperor – probably a weeping third nipple. The couple were divorced early in AD 221, after Heliogabalus had decided to marry the middle-aged Vestal, Aquilia Severa, in a perverse attempt to subjugate Rome's predominant religion to his own.

It's unlikely that Julia Paula ever acquired much power at court, and she would most likely have retired after her marriage to her wealthy father's home. Julius Paulus continued as tutor to Alexander, who Heliogabalus was to adopt as his heir, so the rupture created by the two parties through their divorce was clearly not sufficient to demand that the family go into exile. Independent of Heliogabalus's dismissal of Julia as a woman, the latter would have been denied individual expression in her marriage by the repressive presence of Heliogabalus's grandmother Maesa, and his mother Symiamira, who remained the dominant women in his life.

Heliogabalus's second attempt at márriage constituted as much a social scandal as his relationship with Hierocles. Unethically, he took from her religious community one of the Vestals whose duty it was to tend and preserve the sacred fire which symbolised Rome's existence. In this case, the woman Aquilia Severa seems to have been a hag, expressively unattractive in physical appearance, and as with Julia Paula to have been much older than the youthful Heliogabalus.

The Vestals were a community of patrician women, who even if their virginity was suppositious, lived apart from the world, dressed in white linen, and arranged their hair in six braids to symbolise chastity. They took a prominent part in all public functions, and were the arbiters of moral taste, as well as being consulted on the subject of ethics. Vestals found guilty of fornication were traditionally punished by being buried alive. Aquilia Severa who was the daughter of the jurist Aquilius Sabinus, who had been Prefect of Rome both in AD 214 and 216, was most likely married to Heliogabalus in the spring of AD 221, at a time propitious to celebrate the union between the god Elagabal and Demeter. Although Aquilia was granted the title of Augusta, Heliogabalus seems almost immediately to have realised his error in violating taboo, and to have sent Aquilia back to her community. That he revised his opinion on the damage done and remarried Aquilia the following year goes to demonstrate the emotional confusion at work in Heliogabalus's complex psychology. Fascinated by the mythical qualities of Aquilia Severa, his pact with her was also dominated by the wish to abuse her inviolability. Given that all the coins struck to commemorate her marriage depict her as old and unattractive, it seems likely that Heliogabalus's attraction to Aquilia was founded on a spiritual rather than physical basis. But Heliogabalus would have been only too aware that with a Vestal, even marriage was regarded as incest. Most probably he saw in Aquilia a religious sensibility that in part mirrored his own, only without the shadow content that so dominated Heliogabalus's life.

The cult of Vesta concerned itself with the worship of Jupiter Capitolinus, one of the two spiritual pillars on which the Roman state had been founded. Vesta herself was identified with the cult of the great earth mother, and an image of the goddess Pallas known as the Palladium was kept inside the temple. Heliogabalus desacralized the temple by removing the Palladium from its interior, but we may also read this act of appropriation as a metaphor for the incest implied by his abduction of a Vestal from her order. Whether Heliogabalus committed so flagrant a breach of law as to dishonour the state by removing its tutelary gods to his own temple is open to conjecture, but we can certainly imagine him fired up by the danger of the prospect. And what sort of marriage could have evolved from the union of two figures in such discord? Can we expect Aquilia Severa to have loved the man who had so fundamentally abused her religion? What would their discourse have been other than one of radical disharmony? Heliogabalus's desire to proclaim his own god as supreme throughout the empire would surely have provoked extreme hostility on the part of Aquilia. Aquilia may have had no option but to marry Heliogabalus, but if this was the case, why then did she agree to remarry him the following year? If the marriage had proved untenable, then Aquilia would have been glad of its annulment, and as Heliogabalus appears to have done nothing to honour her family, then the reasons for her marriage were clearly not those of social advance. Nor can we expect of a man accused of debasing his office by openly kissing Hierocles on the penis during the celebrations for the festival of Flora any passionate commitment to Aquilia, and nor as we know it from her inscription was she of an age likely to produce an heir. More likely, if there was a common bond shared by the two, it was formed by the attraction of opposites who nonetheless were possessed of deeply religious sensibilities.

Heliogabalus's third marriage was to Annia Faustina, who was the great-granddaughter of the emperor Marcus Aurelius through his fourth daughter Arria Fadilla. It is assumed that she too was an older woman, between forty and forty-five years of age at the time of her marriage, and from this we can assume that Heliogabalus's attraction to Julia lay more with her imperial connections than with the likelihood of her providing him with children. That Heliogabalus seems in his choice of wives to have been attracted to women who were in effect surrogate mothers is little surprising given his sexual orientation and history of incestuous desires. That Annia was linked by blood to Heliogabalus's cousin, rival and adopted heir Alexander, can have done little to improve a marriage so unstable that it seems to have been dissolved after little more than a matter of months. Annia's biography is insubstantial, with little or nothing known of the role she played at court or in Heliogabalus's life. She was implicated in a plot involving two senators, Silius Messala and Pomponius Bassus, aimed at deposing Heliogabalus, the two men having been noted as notorious conspirators under Caracalla. After attempting to enlist the army for support sometime in the winter of AD 221, the two were apprehended, and as we know it Bassus was tortured and executed for his part in the scheme.

Heliogabalus was moody, paranoid and distrustful throughout the time of his marriage to Annia, and he must have sensed that by marrying an aristocrat he had exposed himself to the vulnerabilities of being an outsider to her class. That Heliogabalus was to remarry Aquilia Severa after his brief, abortive marriage to Annia was a decision so ill-advised as to precipitate the army's turning against him and his own final end.

In his intensely staged, hormonally chaotic years as emperor, Heliogabalus lived with the redshift burnt-out of a pulsar. The tidal flow of his youthful endocrine system that powered him on in the search for sexual ecstasy, was also the force behind his aspirations to godhead. If we separate the two, we do Heliogabalus the injustice of judging him simply as a mortal. We fall into historic categorisation, rather than the reinvention of character through psychological update.

Heliogabalus was by nature a sensual hedonist. Gold was his colour, and he wore it to compensate for the absent sun. The mirrored ceiling above his bed allowed Heliogabalus to see and be seen in the sexual act. He wanted to know himself as a man used as a woman by another man. In the intensity of the moment he was the undisputed sun-god. He was both the light and its source.

Heliogabalus's domestic rituals, and the extravagance he brought to colour-coding his dinners, are legendary. Heliogabalus set a fashion by having his couches covered in gold, and that he gave dinners in various colours, one day a green one, the next a bright blue, a purple, a red, a black, all organised around his inventive culinary aesthetic. The synaesthetic use of colouring food in order to establish a sensory mood to be shared at the table, was a trait also adopted by Nero, Domitian and Commodus. The apparent unnaturalness of each dish was presented in a way that suggested participation in a ritual. The guests were introduced to food as a form of symbolic magic, and by their witnessing rites that were symptomatic of the emperor's taste for the unusual.

We know also that Heliogabalus was the first emperor to have silver cooking-pots and utensils, silver services and vessels said to weigh a hundred pounds and engraved with lewd orgiastic scenes. We are also aware of the alacrity with which his demands were executed. In the duration of his short-term rule, temples were constructed, the palace re-designed according to his aesthetic, and a great deal of jewellery, clothes and household items fashioned for his personal use.

If Heliogabalus was partial to theming a banquet by dictating the colour of.the food to be eaten, then his gourmand tastes were characteristically reserved for the extreme delicacies. In imitation of the gourmet Apicius, he liked to eat camels' heels, cockscombs, and the tongues of peacocks and nightingales, as the latter were thought to provide immunity against the plague. His decadent tastes also favoured a melange of mullets' innards, flamingoes' brains, partridge eggs, thrushes' brains and the heads of parrots, pheasants and peacocks. His food repertoire extended to a love of mullets' beards, served with parsley, kidney-beans and fenugreek, dormice baked in poppies and honey, peacocks' tongues flavoured with cinnamon, oysters stewed in garum, sea-wolves from the Baltic, sturgeons from Rhodes, fig-peckers from Samos and African snails. And in keeping with his love of the unusual Heliogabalus had his wine flavoured with infusions. He had mastic and pennyroyal provide bouquet to red wine, and added ground pine-cones and rose petals to his rosé. He also favoured Mulsum, a drink composed of white wine, roses, absinthe and honey, and imported light wines from Greece, as well as enjoying vintage Falernian. His aesthetic vocabulary was regarded as perverse by his contemporaries, and was to become in time the blueprint to a decadent genre that would find a 19th century literary expression in the works of Baudelaire, Huysmans and Wilde.

Heliogabalus fed his dogs on goose liver, and his horses on grapes from Apamea. He provided parrots and pheasants for his pet leopards and lions. He was fascinated by his tame leopards: he would strike terror in his guests by having them introduced to the room during dinner, the company being unaware that the animals were harmless. The emperor ate wild sows' udders, while his leopards left a trail of undigested parrots' feathers on the floor. A particular favourite at table were deformed men, who Heliogabalus – as fond of freaks as his illustrious predecessors – would invite in sets of eight; the one-eyed, the crippled, and the obese were seated in octagonal configurations to provide bizarre visual entertainment. At one feast a million violets and burgundy-red rose petals were unleashed from above, completely engulfing and suffocating to death the more unfortunate diners.

Heliogabalus had his peas mixed with gold pieces, his lentils with onyx, beans with amber, and rice with pearls. As extravagant as Caligula, who dissolved pearls in vinegar, he regularly sprinkled pearls instead of pepper on fish and mushrooms. His fish were presented sheathed in gold leaf. Yet he was equally capable of paying his friends' yearly salaries with jars of scorpions, frogs or vipers.

Heliogabalus also devised a game of lucky chances, each guest being designated a gift that was written on a spoon. For the fortunate there were ten pounds of gold and for the unfortunate, ten pounds of lead. The award of ten camels or ten ostriches might find as their antithesis ten flies or ten hens' eggs. More extravagant gifts from Caesar might come in the form of eunuchs, sex-slaves, four-horses chariots, saddle horses, mules, a menagerie of big cats, sedan-chairs and four wheelers. Most of the invited would receive a thousand gold pieces and a hundred pounds of silver a head. Heliogabalus had no care with money. He did not equate expenditure with resources. He had no purchase on the reality that an empire must be maintained. He imagined mountains composed out of precious stones, and polished as though they had been cut by a jeweller. And in his imagination there existed jewelled forests in Africa, and lakes which were liquid gold, their surface a thick membrane of residual gold leaf.

Heliogabalus may also be construed as patron saint of prostitutes, and in particular of rent boys. One smoky October night he assembled the entire cast of Rome's female prostitutes in a public building, and addressed them as his people, and proceeded to lecture them on positions and oral intricacies designed for enhanced pleasure. For this lecture he chose to dress as a theatre call-girl, and when on the following night he gave a talk to the city's collective rent boys, he dressed as one of them to identify with his own. Each prostitute was awarded three gold pieces and given Caesar's commendations to continue with their profession. Heliogabalus was fascinated by the interchangeable mix of pleasure and debasement involved in being a prostitute. His own experience of working as a rent boy sucking cocks on the wharves had alerted him not only to the element of danger in submitting to strangers, but also to the romantic ideal of the possibility of meeting the *perfect* stranger. For Heliogabalus, engagement in anonymous sex had resulted in his finding the man who he was to marry. He is also reported to have visited all of Rome's prostitutes in one day, disguised in a muleteer's hood, and to have given them money without demanding any services in return. To the surprised boy or girl, he offered as his parting words, "Don't tell anyone, but

Antoninus is giving you this". The emperor in identifying with his social opposite had achieved another sort of experiential marriage, the union of sanctioned power with rough trade, and absolute authority with unlawful status. The existential realisation that we are by nature everything and nothing, and that both are the same in terms of final ends, was a truth arrived at by Heliogabalus through the dual tensions at work in his life. The exaggerated lifestyle he adopted, with unlimited wealth at his disposal, was also instrumental to having him realise the existence of poverty. Heliogabalus, after all, needed to know one state and to empathise with its opposite as part of his role as the sacrificial god.

As a boy of sixteen, dyed hair turned damp on a foggy day by the Tiber, he would sense the whole assault of life in his nerves at that moment, *his* moment, while the river pushed its muddy undertow downstream to no end, and to no conclusion. What he knew was what no one would know again in the same way: his own individuality as it burnt bright within the context of reality, a god's reality. A body floated by as he stood watching. He would like to have lifted it out by the hair and kissed its slack mouth. If he only raised his hand in the cold fog he knew he would have the sun return. The sun was in him. Orange and red and eternal.

Heliogabalus was by all accounts a zoolatrist. He kept within the palace precincts a variety of creatures including hippopotami, a crocodile, a rhinoceros, panthers, leopards, lions, ostriches and a variety of snakes largely brought to him from Egypt. For reasons of ostentation he would have his chariot drawn by four wolfhounds, or on one occasion by four stags yoked together. At other times it would be lions or tigers which would be used for the same purpose, and always that of dramatically colouring his actions. He once even drove a chariot pulled by four elephants across the Vatican Hill, pounding sacred tombs into dust in the process. And on special occasions Heliogabalus would utilise a chariot team of naked women, whipping their straining buttocks as they hauled him through the twilit streets. He would for the day call himself Mother of the

Gods or *Liber Bacchus*. He would be the presentation of myth to his subjects, dressed in whatever costume was appropriate to the god with whom he identified. Nobody ever forgot Heliogabalus after seeing him, and the acrimonious commentaries on his life as emperor were in part the product of historians anxious to discredit the youth of his better qualities.

Identification by way of empathy with a fantasy persona is a common theme of psychodynamics. We all inhabit plural rather than singular selves, even though the reality of each adopted self remains a subjective one. If we were to believe in the objective reality of our multiple selves, and to attach a value to them at the expense of ego, then we would be considered delusional or schizophrenic. But there is no case for arguing that Heliogabalus was a schizophrene, or that his engagement with metamorphic reality was in any way pathological. Rather he knew his identity only too well. Heliogabalus's bisexual archetype was prompted by the need to insight dionysian madness in everyday functions.

Heliogabalus was only fifteen and sixteen at the time of establishing a refined aesthetic, displaying extraordinary tastes for one so young. By the age of sixteen he was recognised by the Senate and priestly colleges of Rome as *Sacerdos Amplissimus Dei Invicti Solis Elagabili* (high priest of the unconquerable sun god Elagabalus). The deception implicit in this title was that Heliogabalus was of course a god in his own right. He was the sacrificial divinity forced to adopt the role of hierophant to his cult. If he had come out in terms of owning to his true identity, he would have risked suffering immediate rather than delayed assassination. The one contemporary bust of him to survive shows an androgynous face, the eyes large, and the lips full and sensual. The face is suitably immature and expresses both petulance and femininity, as well as the subject's singular devotion to a religious ideal. The peculiar combination of aesthetic and ascetic qualities incorporated into Heliogabalus's nature often personifies the decadent.

In the public baths Heliogabalus always bathed with the women, and made use of their depilatory creams to remove hair from his face and genitals. He liked the ritual of shaving his male lovers' pubes, so that they would appear de-sexed or mutant. His fetishistic attention to body and clothing detail was always that of someone who flexed gender in the interests of identifying with both sexes. Heliogabalus used only gold vessels for voiding his bowels, and his urinals were made of onyx, even the arc of his piss ritualized as a form of alchemy.

No act of the emperor's was allowed to go unceremonialized. Heliogabalus would have gold dust dispensed over his path, as he objected to walking on the common ground. The city's streets would be sanded with gold, as the emperor moved across town in a chariot drawn by naked women, occasionally alighting to pick up an attractive or well-endowed boy or to remark on a florist's extravagantly colourful display. His own rooms professed a continuous shock of roses, while in the spring his demands were for hyacinths and indigo-coloured Parma violets. His innately pacifist and anti-war views must have alarmed his governing contemporaries, and by way of protesting against military manoeuvres he ordered that the fleet should be sunk in the harbour, and that the act should be viewed as a morally liberating one.

Within his own household Heliogabalus liked to occupy the roles of cook, confectioner, perfumer, shopkeeper and pimp. The diversity of these functions not only accommodated Heliogabalus's longings to dress up in drag, but also provided him with the element of play necessary to his theatricalized conception of himself. Transvestites need to be treated like women, and Heliogabalus, apart from affecting a woman's domestic role, urged Hierocles as his husband to slap him and to berate him for his untiring index of infidelities.

At one dinner Heliogabalus served the heads of six hundred ostriches, for the brains to be eaten. He also took a dead whale and weighed it, and is said to have presented the equivalent weight in fish to friends at a banquet. If the emperor's preoccupations with food were on a macrocosmic scale, then we can view his engagement with enormity as a drive towards subverting heroism. Whatever still went into capturing a whale was undermined by the emperor's conversion of the whale into a symbol of gluttony. What is more the whale was substituted by the equivalent weight of edible fish. The role of hunter or fisherman was made redundant by associating the pursuit with the absurd.

The fish Heliogabalus ate were always cooked in blue sauce, as if in seawater, to retain their live colour. His attention to a vocabulary of fetishistic detail was exhaustive, and included practises like never wearing the same garment or the same pair of shoes twice. Heliogabalus adopted the same attitude towards sex, and apart from his relationship with Hierocles pursued a life in which pleasure was taken from quick-encounter sex. In Ovid's *Metamorphoses*, if a god gives himself to a human, the experience is once and once only. Heliogabalus's exalted sense of identity would doubtless have kept him conscious of the need to retain mystique, rather than make himself readily available to the same lover.

Each year at midsummer, Heliogabalus had his sacred black stone carried in great procession from the temple on the Palatine to the huge eastern-style temple built on the edge of the city. The stone itself was transported in a chariot drawn by six white horses, the emperor running backwards in front of the chariot, so as not to turn his back on the god.

The streets had been strewn for the occasion with sand sprinkled with gold dust, and the whole route was lined by crowds carrying torches and throwing flowers in the path of the procession. There were great umbrellas at each corner, and Heliogabalus was supported on either side by minders there to protect him from the crowd. The rear of the procession was kept up by the Equestrian order and the Praetorian guards. The sight of the boy-god emperor running backwards through the cordoned-off streets must have been awesome to the onlookers. Largely out of synch with his religio-cult practises, the spectators would have viewed this ritual as a component belonging to myth. It was also potentially dangerous, an invitation to murder. Heliogabalus's vulnerability was apparent to everyone who watched the slow-motion procession head out to Rome's suburbs.

The curious could already scent his death. There was something about Heliogabalus they observed, which was too flagrantly unorthodox to be accepted by popular taste.

The whole distance he was accompanied by musicians. The band played a variety of instruments ranging from crotalums, which are a form of castanets, to barrel-shaped drums called tambours, to sistrums which are the ancient Egyptian rattle used in the worship of Isis, to silver trumpets called hasosra, as well as the kind of large harp known as nebels. Heliogabalus worked with the music, its rhythm building in him to the pitch of shamanic frenzy. He was a scandal to the people, not because he had the audacity to wear jewels on his shoes, but because he openly celebrated his marriage with death. Heliogabalus may only have been sixteen, but he had travelled a long way out on a trajectory that terminally distanced him from everyday life. He was a madman. A shaman. A ritualist. A religiomaniac. A magician. A pretty boy. A wife. A mythomaniac. A quasi-eunuch.

But he was emperor.

If Heliogabalus prescribed to a particular archetype, then it was in part to the transformative powers associated with Dionysus. Dionysus is the god who provides a gateway to the senses. His cult not only attends the vine, and is identified with drunkenness, but is also a pointer to inspired music, bisexual consciousness, orgy, and a half-prophetic, half-destructive madness. The music created for bacchanalia has the insurgent beat that Heliogabalus demanded of his players. The primitive rhythm was coloured by Berecynthian flutes, mixed with discordant horns, inflected by the lyre and accompanied by the delirious cacophony of bacchanals. It was a music that dubbed a sense of primitive Eastern rites onto a Western aesthetic. To the Syrian-born Heliogabalus who had assumed imperial power at Rome, the music came up in him as the union of two cultures. He liked the incantatory repetition of chant cutting across *extempore* instrumentation. It was a ritual in which anything could happen. People lost their sense of individual identity as the beat persisted, and so barriers were broken down, and what would normally have been conceived as taboo was now sanctioned by ritual. This world of permeable gender definition was Heliogabalus's drug. He was openly male and female. He would have liked to banish patriarchy from Rome, and replace it with its matriarchal equivalent, dangerous and excessive, like the god Dionysus himself.

Heliogabalus's identification with the wine-god was an instance of his transposing a Western archetype to the rites connected with the Eastern sun-god Elagabalus; nor was the return of the repressed god in Heliogabalus simply a prompter to unadulterated excess. Rather, given Heliogabalus's predisposition to religious ceremony, these *orgia* were not so much sexual orgies as acts of devotion, the conduit to a particular kind of religious experience. Inspiration in the sense of the poet feeling possessed or overtaken by his theme is the means of channelling a sensory overload of inner experience into concrete form. Illumination for the poet, as for the dionysian initiate comes by way of being aware of the given message. The expression of madness as an interpretable altered state, rather than a pathological phenomenon is a rite essential to dionysian consciousness. The hard drinking that Heliogabalus did at banquets, and largely in the interest of getting inebriated, was quite separate from the transpersonal intoxication he invited by way of celebrating ritual. Running backwards through the city Heliogabalus in his tranced-out and ecstatic state of communion with the god in his veins, would have been unapproachably numinous. He would have been at that moment Elagabalus-Dionysus. But to the uninitiated the intensely transported youth would have represented the confusion and terror that often comes when Dionysus is present; Dionysus who blurs the boundaries between madness and sanity, male and female, abandon and self-control, the sexual and the psychic, consciousness and unconsciousness.

Heliogabalus embodied all these states and so became the assassin's target. Somebody in the crowd was that very moment visualizing the precise juncture in the youth's neck where the blade would hit and express plumes of glittering arterial blood.

Heliogabalus in his personification of the androgyne represented the perennial inciter to male opposition. The army waited and watched. They were not going to tolerate an emperor who wanted to be a woman, nor one whose fetishes involved pissing into an onyx urinal.

Each time Heliogabalus made himself up as a woman he felt his power increase. Painting his eyebrows and applying kohl to his eyes, he would wear leopardskin as token of the god's instruction. He would orchestrate his own measure of dementia in accordance with the increased hold established by the god. If Dionysus became too prominent he would redress the balance by accentuating the ascendency of Elagabalus. And if he felt like going out and dancing in the street and proclaiming the exhilarative sense of being himself, then Hierocles was there to haul him back and blacken his eyes as a lesson in restraint.

Heliogabalus may be considered quintessentially Ovidian in the way his life reflects metamorphic dualities. And like Tiresias with his special talent for insighting what has happened to him, and in retrospect being able to benefit from the knowledge of having been both sexes, so Heliogabalus more than any other Roman emperor occupies a mythic dimension. He has the ambiguity of Dionysus, now present, now absent; his disguises ensure him a protean rather than fixed identity.

Heliogabalus confused his subjects by his inability to conform to protocol. The army felt threatened by the emperor's lack of ideological muscle. Heliogabalus's largely apolitical stance threatened to undermine the Senate. The emperor was concerned with something far bigger than political dialectics, and that was devotion to spiritual awareness. The state expected of the emperor a concern with secular affairs that he appeared unwilling to give. Heliogabalus was otherwise preoccupied with issues of converting polytheistic Rome to an enforced monotheism. Again he had an ambivalent edge to his quest, for he both was, and was not, the god of his declared worship. Heliogabalus didn't just want to be the reflection of his reflection: he wanted to escape into the mystery of the other. He was already formulating what Rimbaud would later on pronounce of the self: "Je est un autre". His attempted flight to that state was through the senses, or more specifically through being an erotic sensualist.

Heliogabalus existed for himself as mythic consciousness. He lived at a remove from time in the precinct of imagination. When it all got too much for him, he locked himself up with his mother. Sex with her was a preparatory initiation into death. Each time he renegotiated a voyage back to her interior he negated the life principle and reacquainted himself with death. When the end did come he would die in his mother's arms, both of them cut down by precisional assassins, their blood mixed in their final convulsions.

It wasn't just Heliogabalus who lived in a state of crisis. The Roman Empire itself was responding to a tropism of decay, in which a corrupt retro-virus policed a declining organism. Both Tiberius and Caligula had attempted to solve the problem of big estates and dispossessed peasantry by a radical distribution of land, but both had been frustrated in their attempts by the oligarchs, and the senatorial class had resumed its sway. The greed and incompetence of the ruling caste, and the autocratic role adopted by respective Caesars, most of whom were temperamentally unfit to rule, had caused the Empire to implode in a chain of socio-cultural catastrophes.

The wealth of the late republic was dependent on the loot of many wars, on slavery in the plantations, and on provincial labour. The contrast between the hedonistic pursuits of the aristocratic landowners and the abject misery of an institution of slaves was at its most acute. Living largely from a wealth derived from the land the senatorial class were the opponents of any economic expansion which challenged its own position. Heliogabalus didn't seem to care less. He was more concerned about his make-up than politics within the Senate. Moreover he showed an equal disinterest in the gladiatorial games, a lack which would have alienated him in the eyes of Rome's plebeian ranks, who expected nothing less than the total participation of their emperor in those circuses of unadulterated slaughter – although Heliogabalus *did* ensure that all the carnivorous beasts used in the arena were fed a strict diet of live pheasants.

Heliogabalus instead liked to engage in black humour, often bordering on the absurd. He appointed a dancer to prefecture for the guard, and he made Gordius, a charioteer, prefect of the watch, and Claudius, a barber, prefect of the grain-supply.

Professions like that of hairdresser were considered as little more than menial tasks by the aristocracy, and occupations like dancer and charioteer were openly disparaged by the ruling power. That Heliogabalus elevated three men of undesirable status to prime positions can be seen as a deliberate move to promote equality. By endorsing unsanctioned privileges in this manner, Heliogabalus was in fact substituting the heterodox with the unorthodox, the heterosexual ideal with its homosexual counterpart, the regenerate with the degenerate. It was an action that mirrored the cultural entropy at work within the Empire. And that Heliogabalus had no children from his relations with three wives suggests that he may have used women in a sexually unreproductive manner, limiting his congress to enforced sodomy, this reversal of sexual productivity fitting well with his attempts to subvert conventions.

Heliogabalus clearly delighted in degrading office. He appointed a muleteer to take charge of the five per cent tax on inheritances, assisted by a courier, a cook and a locksmith. These anarchic gestures belong not only to the theatre of the absurd, but are examples of an emperor applying favouritism to some of the lowlife he had met through sexual encounters. As when Caligula gave rank to his horse Incitatus, there is something shocking about the nature of these appointments, as though Heliogabalus in his design to celebrate the socially outlawed, was determined to confront the Senate with parodies of its office. By making unsuitable appointments Heliogabalus was in fact pointing up the challenge of a largely unauthorised corruption to an existing one. It is little wonder that his enemies existed in high places. Heliogabalus's flamboyant person and the defiant temerity he showed in undermining a Senate who were no more than absent landowners living off slavery, was bound to trigger a need for vengeance on the part of the existing status quo.

Many of Heliogabalus's sensory indulgences were little different to those of Caligula, Nero or Commodus, and they correspond to a broad-spectrum aesthetic in which obsessive behaviour replaced any notion of a selfless concern with government. In imposing his sexual preferences on the Senate, Heliogabalus was to run the risk of trivializing office by confusing it with pleasures granted his seemingly rampant libido. If a man's genitals were advantageously large, then he would be appointed to a position of power irrespective of his abilities to fill it. The continuous necessity to update established values with their contemporary equivalents is the definition of progress. Heliogabalus was understandably intolerant of any other generation than his own. His methods of shocking his seniors out of complacency were those of equivocal sexuality and the short-fuse tactics of someone enjoying youthful precociousness at the expense of studied conservatism. There is a time to burn and a time to cool, and Heliogabalus was intent on blazing.

As a ritualist Heliogabalus would undoubtedly have participated in the secret rites pertaining to the Mysteries of Eleusis, as well as have been familiar with practises associated with the dionysian or bacchic cults. An initiate to the Eleusinian Mysteries, a succession of esoteric rites archetypally constellated round the myth of Demeter and her ravaged daughter Persephone, abducted and taken to the underworld by Hades, would be witness to a series of mystical dramas performed with the purpose of recreating the myth. Here the hierophant played the role of the Demiourgos, the instructor of the universe, and the Daduchus played Helios, the Epibomios took the part of Selene, the Keryx that of Hermes, and Demeter was represented by her priestesses. And to increase the sense of potent mystery surrounding the hermetic rituals which took place in semi-darkness, there were also monsters and giants constructed as stage-props to heighten the dramatic effects.

The climax to the mysteries would have been the symbolic visitation of the neophyte to the underworld, in which the candidates crowned with myrtle, and carrying a bacchos or thyrsus, would have followed the hierophant's torch through a complex of underground tunnels. At various stations of the journey the initiates would have encountered actors personifying a range of punishments inflicted on the unredeemable. After experiencing what was quite literally a journey through the dark, the neophyte was brought before the telesterion and would discover a bright light streaming through an aperture in the room, and would hear voices accompanied by music on the other side. Without announcement the doors would fly open, and the candidates would be led out into the light to observe actors dressed in white and singing orphic hymns in celebration of the divine. In this instance paradise was conceived as representing the Elysian Fields, in honour of Persephone who at the time of her abduction was said to be picking violets, irises, saffron and hyacinths in a spring meadow. It was when Persephone's attention was drawn to a narcissus, and she was in the act of picking the mythically charged flower, that Hades ruptured the earth with his gold chariot, and despite the girl's violent resistance carried her off to his underworld kingdom.

The story of Persephone's symbolic rape and the subsequent hold that Hades asserted over her – she was licensed to return to the earth for six months each year – would easily have translated itself into Heliogabalus's repertoire of archetypes. The narrative is one that finds distinct analogies with Heliogabalus's own life, in that like Persephone, his individual destiny was cut short by an unmediated act of violence on his youth.[3]

Heliogabalus' main concerns remained spiritual. That his intense devotion to an amalgam of esoteric rites associated with the god Elagabalus were offset by an overriding desire for extravagance, in no way diminishes the seriousness of his religious pursuits. That Heliogabalus found himself saturated in the luxury of a palace which was partly the remains of Nero's *Domus Aurea*, or Golden House, would only have served to reinforce his conviction that his life as spiritual potentate demanded the endorsement of unlimited wealth. And no matter

Nero's crimes, his abuse of power and his sexual notoriety, he still remained an idol to the masses, and indeed the Rome over which Heliogabalus ruled still remembered Nero by placing roses on his grave. There was also the belief common among the people that Nero would return and his second advent was confidently expected.

Nero, emperor from AD 54–68, had been popular among other things for inaugurating the Neronia, a festival of competitions in music, gymnastics, and horsemanship, modelled on the Greek ones, and had opened the porphyry baths attached to the palace to the people. That the imperial palace was built on 125 hectares of land cleared after the Great Fire of AD 64, for which it was suspected that Nero was in part responsible, only enforced the irony of public worship of an oppressor. Nero had succeeded in securing a place in popular consciousness in the way that extreme individuals do, their misdemeanours appearing preferable in time to the less ambitious crimes of their latter day counterparts.

For the brief moment attendant on Heliogabalus's triumphant procession to Rome, the idea that the new emperor could be Nero's reincarnation must have seemed a distinct possibility. Confusion surrounding this possibility was given an added dimension by the fact that Heliogabalus as the newly acclaimed emperor was ensconced in Nero's former palace. This was a building so sumptuous that the interior walls were studded with jewels, the dining-rooms had ceilings of fretted ivory, and there were ventilation systems designed to circulate scented air throughout the building. The main banquet hall was circular and the ceiling rotated day and night like the heavens. It was a domed octagonal room, with the ceiling revolving by water-power. Some of the floors in the palace were malachite, and there were crystal columns and expansive halls painted red and gold. The vestibule had been built to house a statue of Nero 37 metres high, and the place was surrounded by cultivated park land. Nero had invested in the building at a time of financial optimism when he believed that a vast hoard of treasure, deposited by Queen Dido of Carthage centuries before, was recoverable from huge caves in Africa. When the emperor's fantasy failed to materialise Nero had found himself without the finances to continue work on the Golden House. Heliogabalus had paid close attention to the detailed extravagances associated with Nero's reign, and had in many ways attempted to emulate Nero's worst excesses. Heliogabalus not only identified with Nero, but intended to impersonate the dead emperor's ostentatious idiosyncrasies.

Nero's notorious bisexual practises may well have encouraged Heliogabalus in his desire to authorise homosexual marriage. In his love of the charioteer, Hierocles, Heliogabalus would have been aware of the precedent established by Nero in his relationship with the boy Sporus. Nero attempted to transsexualize Sporus by having him castrated, and then married the youth in a ceremony in which Sporus was dressed in clothes normally worn by an Empress. That Heliogabalus was to copy Nero's gay marriage, and that he himself wished to change his sex suggests an almost overstated degree of empathy on his part with his legendary predecessor.

Heliogabalus also knew of Nero's indefinitely prolonged feasts, the orgiastic nature of which involved the guests selecting male or female prostitutes as a distraction between courses. Nero by way of manifesting the extraordinary powers at his disposal would create sensational extravaganzas. Whenever he sailed down the Tiber to Ostia, or cruised past Baiae, he had temporary brothels erected along the shore, where women of high birth, pretending to be prostitutes, waited to solicit and service him and his friends. When Nero travelled he had a train of 500 carriages in attendance, and Heliogabalus with the intention of outrivalling his hero increased the number to 600, justifying this outlandish retinue by claiming that the King of Persia was often accompanied by a train of 10,000 camels.

Heliogabalus's personal expenditure during his reign is estimated as being in the region of £400 million, a sum that suggests he probably spent in excess of £100 million a year funding his private schemes. Only Caligula and Nero before him had burnt money with the same reckless self-indulgence, and with an equally contemptuous disdain for the state. Heliogabalus was capable of having a mountain of snow created for him in his orchard, so that he could find refuge there from the torrid summer heat. We hear also of houses, baths, and huge salt-water lakes built for him in the mountains, and of Heliogabalus ordering that these temporary shelters should be destroyed as soon as he had moved on to his next destination. This practice was intended as a sign to the people that the emperor's individual destiny was like no other's, and that his passage was marked by a spectacular assemblage of events that announced the marvellous. The black column of smoke coiling from the cracked shell of one of Heliogabalus's mountain villas, after he and his retinue had moved on, must have constituted a powerful sign to his contemporaries. Conjecture on the part of the local inhabitants as to the rites acted out on what had become an incinerated disaster-site, would have contributed greatly to the legend surrounding Heliogabalus's Syrian origins and the form of religion he practised. Heliogabalus was viewed not only as a sexual aberrant, but was considered by the superstitious to be an adept to the black arts, with all the intimations of child sacrifice associated with such status.

Heliogabalus not only venerated Nero, but used his biography as the subtext for his lifestyle. Heliogabalus was to employ Nero's life as a metaphor for his own unstintingly constructed forays into licentiousness. Essentially benign and without Nero's unabated capacity for cruelty, it was the decadent and the sensational in Nero that appealed to Heliogabalus, rather than the vicious and homicidal. If Heliogabalus intended to shock it was more in the way of subverting sexual ethics, rather than by committing the atrocities attributed to Nero.

Nero raped the Vestal Virgin Rubria, whereas Heliogabalus less shockingly defied sacred custom by demanding that the Vestal Aquilia Severa should marry him, in the interests of incorporating the worship of Vesta into that of Elagabal. Scandalous as Heliogabalus's actions were in this respect, they were less offensive than Nero's outright violation of Rome's high priestess, and one can only speculate that Heliogabalus's misconceived conduct was in some way attributable to his desire to emulate Nero by possessing a traditionally unobtainable woman.

Nero kicked his pregnant wife Poppaea to abortion and bloody death, but afterwards turned his attention to the boy Sporus because he resembled Poppaea in appearance. And Heliogabalus too in his relations with his homosexual lovers seems to have tried to recreate female characteristics within the male.

Nero, dressed in a lion's skin, would attack the genitals of women and men bound naked to stakes. He not only proceeded to murder his mother Agrippina, and his aunt Domitia Lepida, but he ordered the execution or voluntary suicide of almost anyone he considered a rival. Even his old and revered tutor Cicero, was forced to commit suicide after Nero refused him the right to retire from public life.

Any abominations on Heliogabalus's part were mainly attributable to religious practises, his assassination of Gannys notwithstanding. His was a self-regarding reign in which affairs of state were sacrificed to those of personal obsession. If Heliogabalus's sexual politics were considered outrageous, then so were his attitudes towards war, or rather his disinclination to become involved in military affairs. When the possibility arose for Heliogabalus to assert himself as a commander by having the army advance against the Marcomanni, the inhabitants of Bavaria and Bohemia, he remained unwilling to initiate an offensive. When he was told that the Marcomanni had been subdued by Commodus by means of Chaldean magic, and that to remove the spells would have the Marcomanni resume war, he was only too delighted to accept this as a reason for inaction.

Certainly both Nero and Heliogabalus possessed oedipal traits, and both would seem to have had incestuous relationships with their mothers. But no matter the complex machinations at work within the emperor's inner circle, and the always opportunistic conspiracies abroad to depose Caesar, it's difficult to imagine that Heliogabalus would ever have turned on his mother with the vengeance that Nero showed Agrippina. After having tried repeatedly to poison Agrippina, whose antidotes dispelled each renewed attack, and after finally arranging for her to be murdered, Nero showed a necrophiliac interest in her corpse. Nero and his gloating circle examined the dead body for its good and bad points, remarking between drinks on the virtues of the legs, hips, arms, anus and vagina, and handling the corpse as though they were appraising a potential lover. This complete absence of remorse for having killed Agrippina, and the dispassionate objectivity Nero displayed in reviewing his mother's corpse, suggests a sensibility at a radical remove from Heliogabalus's emotional dependency on his mother, and his more strained relationship with his grandmother.

But that Nero experienced some degree of guilt for the part he had played in murdering Agrippina was evident by the fact that his dead mother haunted his dreams. Nero complained that he was being pursued by the furies, and unable to free himself of their menacing presence he employed Persian occultists to conjure up the ghost and take measures to expel it. Nero developed sleep-fright as a consequence of matricide, and we can imagine his nights as a tormented insomniac, desperately trying to find release from his visions through alcohol and narcotics.

Both emperors displayed a religious fetishism; Nero despised all religious cults except that of Atargatis, the Syrian goddess, but in a fit of temper he urinated on her divine image, as a means of expressing his superiority. After abandoning his devotion to Atargatis he remained faithful to the worship of the statuette of a girl sent him anonymously as a talisman against conspiracies. He is said to have worshipped the girl as though she were a powerful goddess, and to have sacrificed to her three times a day, expecting people to believe that she communicated to him a knowledge of the future.

Heliogabalus's conception of the divine would never have permitted him to urinate on the sacred image, a defiance of taboo that illustrates much about the perverse themes at work in Nero's psyche. Heliogabalus's religious drive was directed towards the concretization of the sacred, whereas Nero's intentions were aimed at the desacralization of any image which appeared to challenge his own claims to divinity.

Heliogabalus also drew inspiration for his decadent lifestyle from the life of Caligula. More extreme than Heliogabalus in the need to proclaim himself a god, Caligula built a temple to himself on the Palatine, and housed in it a life-sized gold image which was dressed every day according to the clothes he happened to be wearing. This act of unpopular self-veneration was to lose Caligula support, and was a monomaniacal gesture altogether lacking in the profound spirituality that we associate with Heliogabalus. Caligula would also talk confidentially with a statue of Jupiter Capitolinus, alternately cajoling and abusing the image, and placing his ear to the god's mouth in anticipation of a reply.

Heliogabalus also found in Caligula a prototypical cross-dresser, whose transvestism did as much to shock his contemporaries as Heliogabalus's own excursions into unashamed drag. Caligula often appeared in public in embroidered cloaks covered with precious stones, and would sometimes wear a woman's silk dress. Caligula had a fetish for army boots, particularly the kind worn by his body-guard, but felt equally comfortable in women's flat shoes. He would dye his beard gold, and hold in his hand a thunderbolt, a trident, or a caduceus, as symbols of the gods. As a style later adopted by Heliogabalus, Caligula would dress up as Venus and impersonate her in his homosexual relations with Marcus Lepidus.

If Heliogabalus was highly sexed, something that may have been attributable to his age, then Caligula was easily his libidinal counterpart. The spectrum of Caligula's sexual rapacity extended to his four wives, incest with his sisters, a notorious passion for the prostitute Pyrallis, as well as an active gay life. Heliogabalus's obsession with penis size in his male lovers suggests a more specialized repertoire in comparison with Caligula's sex addiction. Whatever Heliogabalus's natural delight in extravagance, he must have thrilled at the idea of being an understudy to Nero's and Caligula's unprecedentedly self-indulgent spending. Caligula rapidly liquidated Tiberius's entire fortune of 27 million gold pieces, a consumption of money that Heliogabalus was to emulate in his compulsive need to demolish the imperial fortune. Caligula's disrespect for wealth led him to stand on the roof of the Julian Basilica and fist money and jewels at the passers-by. He also built customised Liburnian pleasure boats, equipped with ten banks of oars, jewelled decks, multi-coloured sails, and incorporating swimming pools, marble colonnades and banqueting halls below deck. Caligula also had the idea of constructing arboretums on these personalised craft, and took an interest in cultivating vines and a variety of apple trees on board.

Nero prided himself most on his voice, and accompanying himself on the lyre, would perform for hours in front of arbitrarily packed theatre audiences. He experienced genuine stage fright and anxiety before performing, and extended his recital for such long periods that women in the audience were known to give birth, while men even risked dropping down from the wall at the rear to escape from the tedium of the performance. His extreme jealousy of the other contestants, and his desire to detract from the merits of previous winners, rings true to his megalomaniacal behaviour. He would accordingly demolish the statues and busts of those who had excelled in the same art, and have them dragged away with hooks and dumped in sewers.

It is unclear whether Heliogabalus's voice was the high-pitched falsetto of a queen, or whether perhaps it achieved that register only at times of inner crisis, when a separation between masculine and feminine components was most acutely experienced. Heliogabalus doubtless modulated his voice in the attempt to give it masculine authority, no matter its telling feminine signature. He certainly sang, but unlike Nero who attached such great significance to his singing voice, we are given no account of its timbre or characteristic tone, of whether he sang arias like a diva, or performed songs of intimate poetry. His musical gifts certainly extended to playing the pipes, the horn and the pandura, and also to performing on the organ.

Heliogabalus as much as Caligula and Nero seems to have been impelled to act in a way that would ensure he was remembered by posterity. The need to overreach himself by sexual notoriety can also be seen as the attraction to acquiring mythic status. And indeed, his name is still used as a byword for homosexual transgression, and the orgiastic lifestyle in which he indulged. By dissociating from the norms of social life like family, and accepted religion, Heliogabalus lives on in the role of sexual outlaw, a radical who opposed sociological and ideological conventions, and yet remained emperor for four years.

Throughout his precarious reign Heliogabalus faced a series of rebellions and uprisings invariably triggered by the low esteem in which he was held by the army. As early as AD 218 the third legion "Gallica", stationed in Syria, decided to defect from the youth it had so erroneously championed, and there was an unsuccessful move to make Verus, their commander, emperor. Subsequent attempts to depose Heliogabalus by the Fourth Legion, by the fleet, and by a pretender called Seleucus were also suppressed in the interests of maintaining civic peace. But Heliogabalus was criticized even amongst his own circle for his imprudence in appointing dilettantes to important positions of state. One such example of aberrant judgement was the appointment of Publius Valerius Comazon to the position of commander of the Praetorian Guard in AD 218, a man whose family may have been professional stage artists, and who was therefore considered to be of low social origins. The army never forgot this insult to its credibility, nor ever forgave the emperor for jeopardising the empire's stability by having it governed by inept favourites, elected purely on the merits of penis size, who commanded nothing but disrespect from their subordinates. It was as a means of trying to reverse the damage he had done to the empire in this respect that Heliogabalus was advised in AD 221 to adopt his young cousin Alexander Severus, and designate him Caesar, son, and heir. This boy of 13, Bassianus Alexianus, was born on 1 October AD 208 at Arca Caesarea in Phoenicia, and was popular with the praetorian guard, even though his mind came under the dominating influence of his mother, Julia Mamaea. If the adoption on Heliogabalus's part was a move intended to silence the army, the sexual admission implied by the act is not without significance. In the same year as Heliogabalus adopted his cousin, Alexander, he married Annia Faustina, a descendant of Marcus Aurelius and the widow of a man the emperor had recently put to death. Heliogabalus may have found himself briefly attracted to Annia for the perversity implied by her marrying her husband's executioner. It is doubtful that intimacy could have existed in so lugubrious a bond.

Heliogabalus's relations with Alexander, who he adopted in the last year of his life, were understandably manipulative and strained. Alexander was popular with the equestrian order, for they observed in him the qualities of quiet spirituality and dignified calm that were so lacking in Heliogabalus. Even though Alexander was only 13 at the time of his adoption, his manner of philosophic restraint in addressing matters of government and the selflessness with which he hinted he would rule were reassuring tokens to an army reproachful of Heliogabalus's religious fanaticism.

When Heliogabalus learnt of Alexander's popularity with the Senate and the praetorian guard, he made it known that he regretted the adoption and would take measures to annul it. Reacting hysterically to his rival, Heliogabalus ordered mud to be smeared on the inscriptions of all statues raised to Alexander in the camp, a gesture of debasement usually directed at tyrants, and one calculated to anger the army.

As if these ill-advised measures against his adopted cousin were not sufficient to appease Heliogabalus's desire for vengeance, he set about scheming to have Alexander murdered. Heliogabalus's plan was to withdraw to the Gardens of Spes Vetus, having left his mother in the palace, together with his grandmother and cousin. From the Spes Vetus gardens Heliogabalus ordered the assassination of a young man, who was held in high esteem by the Senate, as a warning to Alexander. Having achieved his aim, Heliogabalus then offered the promise of rewards to his minders if they would kill Alexander either in the baths, or by poison, or assassination. That word was out to take Alexander's life, and that Heliogabalus's contracted killers were about to move in on their target, was leaked to the Praetorian guard, who in Heliogabalus's absence arrived at the palace and took the boy into custody at the camp.

A contingent of soldiers moved in on the Garden where Heliogabalus was in the act of making preparations for a chariot-race. The emperor, fearing for his life, went into hiding in his residence there, and concealed himself beneath a curtain in the corner of a room. Heliogabalus was saved from instant death by Antiochianus, one of the prefects, who by reminding the soldiers of their oath of allegiance, persuaded them to spare Heliogabalus's life.

But back at the camp the army informed Antiochianus, who was acting as mediator on the emperor's behalf, that they would spare Heligabalus only on condition that he expelled his gay entourage from the palace, and in particular that he removed Hierocles, Gordius and Myrismus from office, and from his personal company. This attempt on the army's behalf to purge Heliogabalus's household of a retinue of undesirables was a last attempt go have the emperor clean up his lifestyle. The terms dictated to Heliogabalus were nothing less than a charged threat: change or die. And that the emperor was incapable of the former meant that his assassination was now just a matter of time.

Heliogabalus was given no choice but to renounce his intimate circle, although he urgently petitioned the army to be allowed to resume his relationship with Hierocles. Even though he was not permitted to have his lover reside at the palace, Heliogabalus continued to meet Hierocles at friends' houses, and with their bond intensified by the imminent prospect of death the two young men learnt to love inside the charged precinct of borrowed time. And on the *kalends* of January, when Heliogabalus and Alexander had been designated joint consuls, he refused to appear in public with his cousin. Informed by his grandmother and mother that the army were threatening to kill him unless he showed proper respect for his cousin, Heliogabalus nominated an urban praetor to represent him at the intended ceremonies at the Capitol, and so refused to make any form of public reconciliation with Alexander. It was a decision that typified his perversity, and one that was to contribute to the brutal manner of his death. Heliogabalus the obstinate. The perverse. The uncompromising. The affronting bitch. The god who dies young. The inverted Adonis from whose blood a dark red flower grows.

Heliogabalus' reign came to an end in March, AD 222. The army rose against Heliogabalus after he had ordered the arrest of those who were known to favour Alexander. Heliogabalus had already acted against his own interests in conceding to the army each time they had dictated that Alexander's powers be restored. That Heliogabalus was known to dislike confrontation, and that he had climbed down on each occasion the army had stood up to him, had led the troops to disrespect the emperor for being cowardly. He had no standing with them. He was considered by the soldiers to be a woman in a man's body. A gender travesty who had disgraced his rank.

Before the soldiers reached Heliogabalus, who was hiding in a stinking latrine outside the palace, they killed his closest friends. Aurelius Eubulus was torn to pieces by the insurgent mob, so was Fulvius the city prefect, and the two Praetorian prefects who supported Heliogabalus. Hierocles was castrated, sodmised by swords and butchered, as were the other gays in Heliogabalus's intimate circle. Naturally, there was no legitimacy to endorse any of these crimes. These were the injustices committed by a self-empowered majority on a defenceless minority, an atrocity in true keeping with the traditions of the Roman Empire.

Heliogabalus and his mother were brutally pulled out of hiding, and quickly despatched in a murderous frenzy. But their anger was still on overdrive, and the soldiers dragged Heliogabalus's decapitated body through the streets, and further insulted it by thrusting it into a putrid sewer. With their frenzy still unappeased, the soldiers retrieved the body, coated in blood and excrement, from the constricted sewer, attached a weight to it to assure that it would sink, and threw the corpse from the Aemillian Bridge into the Tiber. This act ensured that Heliogabalus would never be granted the honour of burial. Heliogabalus was dubbed the "Tiberine", the "Dragged" and "The Filthy" after his ignoble death, the names signifying the sort of sex he had practised.[4]

Heliogabalus's crime was that he was different, he was a transvestite, an ambi-sexual whose open predilection was for sex with men with enormous genitals, and he had introduced an eldritch and unpopular god to Rome. Yet that Heliogabalus inherited a degenerate empire was symptomatic of the times. In brief, the lessening of the empire's productive power by the plague of AD 167, the mega-extravagances of Commodus and Nero, the overambitious enterprises undertaken by Severus, Caracalla's reckless liberality to the army and Macrinus' military failures had all combined to exhaust the revenues. As an uncontrollably big spender Heliogabalus had prevented any chance of financial recuperation. His rapacity for personal expenditure had come at precisely the wrong time, and this allied to his raging eccentricities was an untenable and fatal combination. The teenage sun-god was ultimately eclipsed by his own divinity in a cataclysm of cosmic violence.

Heliogabalus – the divine purple whore, the crowned anarchist – had indelibly scared his lavish ejaculation of solar semen and revolutionary sexuality deep into the anally dark pages of Rome's pulsating history of atrocity and carnage for all recorded time.

1. Rome had known other prominent transvestites, including Clodius Pulcher (a.k.a. Pretty Boy). In 62 BC, Pulcher had created a scandal by disguising himself as a woman in order to participate in the Bona Dea ceremonies, a festival exclusive to women, and attended by the Vestal Virgins and other prominent women in Rome. That year, the festival happened to be held in Julius Caesar's home, and his mother Aurelia spotted Pulcher's indiscretion. Matters were made worse by the rumour that Caesar's wife Pompeia had slept with Clodius on the night in question. Such was Caesar's jealousy that a man dressed in drag should have had so powerful a hold on his wife, that he divorced her for not being above suspicion. Pulcher survived the controversy, but was later knifed to death in a gang battle on the Via Appia.

2. It is reported that in the course of this ritual child butchery Heliogabalus would plunge his hands up to the forearm into the steaming viscera of his sacrificial human victims, seeking divine communion in the same way as Gilles de Rais, a spiritual inheritor of the Roman atrocity genome, would do with his victims over a thousand years later.

3. Heliogabalus' ritual activity also encompassed the *taurobolium*, an initiation ceremony at which bull's blood was poured over the neophyte. Heliogabalus's connection to the bull as a symbol of ritual sacrifice is clear, as the animal featured not only in the rites of Mithraism – a homoerotic solar cult which closely paralleled his own – but in those associated with Cybele. Heliogabalus had so wished to transpose the sacred images affiliated with Cybele from her temple to his own, that he had hoped to win the favours of the priests by personally sacrificing bulls to the goddess. But to be admitted to these rites, the initiate had to undergo castration, or a form of *faux* castration (it seems unlikely that the operation was actually performed, despite Heliogabalus's earlier request to be degenitalised in the interests of becoming a woman).

4. There is a Bacchic legend that tells us that Bacchus or Dionysus, while participating in orgiastic rites was captured by the Titans and torn in pieces. The similarities between the god's self-destructing frenzy – he is dismembered by homicidal mania proportionate to his own degree of intoxication – and Heliogabalus's genderbending provocation of the army are highly significant. Amongst the symbols of this particular mystery given to us by Arnobius are dice, a mirror, tops, rotating wheels and apples taken from the Hesperides. Of particular importance is the symbol of the mirror, created by Vulcan for Bacchus, so that he would recognize himself as representational image. But Bacchus after seeing his image in the mirror went in search of himself everywhere, and considering himself to be plural, developed multiple personalities, and so was ripped apart by the Titans. The creation of polymorphic selves, often associated with hearing voices, is a common

schizophrenic trait, and one that could in this instance account for Bacchus's confusion over his identity. Unable to integrate his fragmented selves, Bacchus relies on altered states to help him shift consciousness. Making himself and his followers delirious from music and drink, Bacchus is then hunted down and killed by the Titans in a way that recalls Heliogabalus's murder. Bacchus too comes under suspicion for his bisexuality, his liberal morals, his unconventional manner of dress, his sexual cult and his partying nightlife. His sacrifice naturally invites comparisons with both Orpheus and Osiris as well as the ritual castration of Heliogabalus.

POSTSCRIPT
"ULTIMA VERBA":
THE FINAL ATROCITY

The slaughter of Heliogabalus's successor, the puny mummy's boy Alexander Severus, by his own troops in AD 235 signalled a precipitous plunge into chaos and near-anarchy. For its final three centuries, the decaying Roman Empire reeled in a grotesque delirium of maledictions, imperial butchery and terminal humiliation. Occasionally, a brutal military strongman would seize the role of emperor and manage to cling onto it for a few years before being bloodily deposed; but mostly, the emperors were slaughtered in rapid succession, propelling the Empire into a frenzied rhythm of carnage, towards its ultimate decimation. In one year alone, AD 238, six different emperors successively held power, with five being swiftly massacred: the majestic Empire transformed itself into one great, steaming bloodbath. The plebeian scum in the urban centres came under the sway of magicians and prophets of apocalyptic doom, who travelled from Judea, Egypt and other sources of ferment, foretelling the disintegration of the Empire and casting virulent curses upon its ruler. In their prophecies, the Roman emperor stands at the centre of a seething chaos, demanding divine adulation as he ceaselessly mutates between the shape of a lethal serpent and that of the Antichrist; then, warrior kings arise from beyond the reaches of the Empire, and shatter its power, unleashing rivers of blood, fire, plague and, ultimately, instituting the total fall of darkness upon the Empire. The prophecies captivated the attention of the urban plebeian scum, who now sadly lacked any viscerally satisfying entertainment.

Rome's last great arena spectacle took place in AD 244, in an atmosphere of undirected, haywire brutality. All of the beasts in the arena's zoo were unceremoniously herded into the killing zone and butchered wholesale; the gladiators compulsively massacred one another to the last man, while the spectators wept. The final gladiator then faced the crowd and sliced his own throat. After that, the abandoned arena fell into total dereliction.

The imperial frontiers became increasingly assailed, ready to burst open on all sides as the Teutonic hordes and the Asian despots prepared to finally obliterate the Roman Empire; the dispirited, faction-ridden legions at the borders grew increasingly mutinous as they tried to stem the inevitable flood. Finally, in AD 408, the rampaging Teutons – held back for centuries – unleashed a massive assault and poured through the frontier; the Visigoth tribe and then the Vandals subjugated the Empire's capital. Rome would be invaded, destroyed and pounded into oblivion on innumerable occasions over the following century. The brutalized and terrorized plebeian scum were sent fleeing for their lives in every direction, and Rome lost large swathes of its population. In AD 476, the last emperor, Romulus Augustulus, was nonchalantly deposed by a pack of mercenaries. The ruined, dirt-encrusted city subsided into decomposition, still echoing in its emptiness with the glorious acts of Caligula and Commodus.

The most abject humiliation in the disintegrating history of the Empire came when the emperor Valerian's army was ambushed and destroyed in AD 260 by the great Persian despot, King Shapur I; the emperor himself was put into chains and taken into captivity to the city of Ctesiphon, on the banks of the river Tigris, where Shapur had his palace. With the emperor at his mercy, Shapur decided that some appropriate degradation was now in order. He began to use Valerian as a human footstool, and when mounting his horse, he would compel the emperor to go down on his hands and knees, so that Shapur could stand on his back while climbing onto the horse. Shapur had decreed that while Valerian was in that position, every citizen of his kingdom, down to the lowliest freaks, morons and beggars, had the inalienable right to bugger the Roman emperor to their heart's content. It has been suggested that dogs, too, possessed this right and exercised it on occasion, but, given the Persian despot's notoriously strict views on abnormal sexual acts, this may be an exaggeration. When, after many years of captivity, the decrepit emperor – who had grown fully accustomed to his role, and even preferred it to his former duties – finally died of old age, Shapur ordered that the entire skin be carefully removed from Valerian's body, all in one piece, before being decorated with abstract patterns in coloured inks. He then hung the emperor's skin on the wall of his palace, as an attractive interior decoration.

The Roman Empire was now plummeting in insane freefall, heading rapidly towards its bitter end. In Rome itself, the disabused citizens experienced no nostalgia whatsoever for the rule of the most inept, butchery-crazed series of tyrants that the western world has ever seen. The Dark Ages were approaching fast, but for a moment at least, the inhabitants of Rome could breathe a sigh of relief and tell one another that now, it was time for *la dolce vita*.

NOTES ON SOURCES

This account is drawn from contemporary sources, biographies, manuals, polemics and newly-excavated documents (notably the "Butrinte Caligula"), as well as from works of the following centuries, from the golden era of Roman scholarship in Germany in the 1900s-1910s, and – least usefully by a wide margin – from recent biographies of Caligula and Commodus. All material of every kind written on the Roman era, whatever its date of composition, reflects the strictures and gaps and limitations of its time, and it would require the most omniscient oracle to say definitively what was authentic.
—*Stephen Barber*

My reconstruction of Heliogabalus's life owes a debt of gratitude to John Stuart Hay's *The Amazing Emperor Heliogabalus*, and to Orma Fitch Butler's studies in *The Life Of Heliogabalus*. Anthony Birley's *Lives Of The Later Caesars* and Antonin Artaud's *Héliogabale, ou L'Anarchiste Couronné* also proved invaluable sources of reference. There is no definitive life of Heliogabalus, and I have attempted to resassemble aspects of his character most likely to resonate in the current times.
—*Jeremy Reed*

INDEX

Alexander Severus, emperor 120, 123, 145, 146, 147, 148, 153
Alexandria 110
    atrocity at 106
Antonius Pius, emperor 10
Artaud, Antonin 19–21, 22, 156
Augustus, emperor 5, 8, 24, 36, 41, 73
Bacchus 150–151
Baudelaire, Charles 107, 125
bestiality 9, 23, 27, 67
buggery, sodomy 5, 9, 24, 26, 27, 28, 31, 33, 34, 35, 40, 45, 46, 47,
    50, 51, 54, 61, 66, 72, 75, 92, 93, 94, 96, 103, 104, 111, 116, 135, 155
Blake, William 19
Britain 29, 38, 41, 42, 56, 103
Caesar, Julius 17, 70, 150
Caesonia 37, 39, 48, 50, 51, 52, 56
Caligula, emperor 5, 6, 7, 8, 11, 12, 13, 14–15, 17, 18, 21, 23–57, 59,
61, 62, 63, 69, 70, 73, 77, 93, 94, 97, 98, 100, 101, 102, 103, 104, 105, 113,
    125, 134, 135, 136, 139, 143–144, 145, 154, 156
    accession of 27–28
    assassination of 15
    deification of 45
Caracalla, emperor 6, 11, 106, 107, 108, 109, 111, 114, 115, 116, 123, 149
carrion man, the 81
castration, emasculation 11, 15, 89, 101, 106, 112, 118, 139,
    148, 150, 151
chariots, chariot-racing 16, 37, 38, 82, 90–92, 97, 98, 100, 105, 110,
    113, 117, 120, 126, 127, 129, 130, 135, 137, 139, 147
Christians, christianity 104
    torture of 6, 8–10
Claudius, emperor 5, 6, 25, 33, 44, 51, 52, 56–57
Commodus, emperor 5, 7, 8, 10, 11, 12–13, 15, 16–17, 93–107, 115, 124,
    136, 141, 149, 154, 156
    accession of 95
    assassination of 105
crucifixion 9, 36, 46, 74, 75

Cybele, cult of 8, 150
Diadumenus, emperor 109, 110
de Rais, Gilles 150
decapitation, beheading 6, 9, 26, 33, 47, 49, 55, 62, 74, 77, 80, 87, 91, 98, 99, 109, 148
Didius Julianus, emperor 106
Dionysus, dionysian rites 47, 128, 131–132, 133, 136, 150
Domitian, emperor 6–7, 8, 10, 11, 12, 124
Drusilla (sister of Caligula) 25, 27, 28, 31, 33, 35, 36
Drusilla (daughter of Caligula) 37, 39, 49, 50, 51, 52, 56–57
dwarfs 6, 8, 31, 48, 80–81
Elagabalus, cult of 107, 108, 111, 114, 115, 118, 121, 128, 132, 133, 137, 140
Eleusis, mysteries of 136–137
fellatio, cock-sucking 5, 64, 65, 66, 67, 68, 111, 113, 126
freaks 6, 8, 31, 33, 44, 48, 63, 80, 97, 125, 155
Galba, emperor 6
Gannys 111–112, 141
Gemellus 25, 27
Geta, emperor 106
gladiators, gladiatorial games 10, 16, 17, 24, 28, 31, 33, 36, 43, 45, 48, 49, 52, 57, 59–92, 93, 96, 97, 98–100, 101, 102, 104, 105, 134, 154
    dwarf 6
    female 6
Great Fire of Rome 8, 138
Hadrian, emperor 10
Heliogabalus, emperor 5, 11, 12, 13, 14, 15, 16, 17, 19–21, 107–151, 153, 156
    accession of 110–111
    assassination of 148–149
    and human sacrifice 114, 115, 150
Hierocles 117, 120, 121, 122, 129, 130, 133, 139, 147, 148
Huysmans, J.K. 12, 125
Incitatus 37, 46, 135
Julio-Claudian dynasty 12, 24, 25, 55, 56, 73, 84, 88, 94, 97
Lucius Verus, emperor 10
Macrinus, emperor 100, 107, 108, 109, 110, 112, 115, 116, 149
Macro 27
magic, magicians 8, 17, 19, 29, 32, 43, 44, 62, 71, 86, 89, 90, 124, 131, 141, 153
Marcus Aurelius, emperor 10, 94–95, 96, 103, 110, 122, 146
Marquis de Sade 5
Mithras, cult of 150

necrophilia   89, 142
Nero, emperor   5, 6, 8, 11, 12, 13, 15, 17, 21, 34, 47, 61, 63, 117,
                  124, 136, 137, 138–139, 140, 141, 142, 143, 144, 145, 149
Nerva, emperor   10
Otho, emperor   6
Ovid   17, 18, 130, 133
Pol Pot   102
Poppaea (wife of Nero)   141
prostitutes, concubines   5, 6, 7, 8, 12, 16, 39, 48, 61, 64, 66, 68, 69,
                                   70, 92, 111, 117, 126, 139, 143
Publius Helvius Pertinax, emperor   105
Pulcher, Clodius a.k.a. Pretty Boy   150
rent boys   16, 17, 113, 126
Rimbaud, Arthur   115, 133
Romulus Augustulus, emperor   154
Saint Blandina, execution of   8, 9
semen, sperm   8, 26, 27, 28, 36, 45, 54, 59, 66, 67, 68, 69, 70,
                                          72, 83, 92, 105, 149
Septimus Severus, emperor   106, 115, 149
taurobolium   150
Teutons   23, 29, 38, 39, 40, 45, 71, 88, 89, 94, 96, 154
Tiberius, emperor   5, 6, 7, 11, 13, 15, 17–18, 21, 24–27, 28, 30, 32,
                                    34, 41, 56, 63, 70, 73, 134, 144
Titus, emperor   8
Trajan, emperor   10
transsexuality   11, 15, 113, 118, 139
transvestism   11, 112, 113, 116, 118, 120, 129, 143, 149, 150
Valerian, emperor   154–155
Vespasian, emperor   8
Vestal Virgins   6, 17, 120, 121, 122, 140, 150
Vitellius, emperor   5, 8, 12
Wilde, Oscar   125

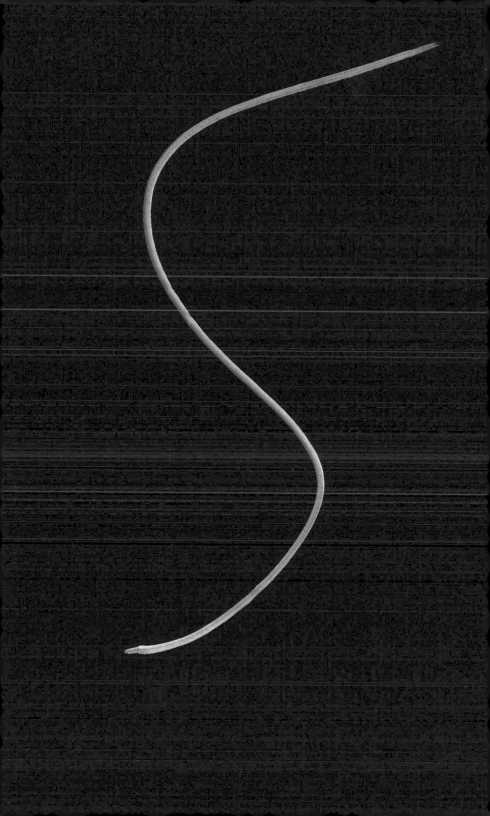